THE INDOMITABLE FREEDOM QUEST

Honoring America's Sacred Trust

Richard D. Cheshire, Ph.D.

Notable Out Takes: A Back Story

From **PRESIDENT RONALD REAGAN**—honorary chairman of the Shakespeare Globe Centre of North America while I was its executive director—a warm handshake and a pat on the back outside his office in LA while we waited off camera for a video shoot to promote our program of classical theater across the country. I barely had time to brief him on his lines as he spun favorite tales of good times with British friends. Reagan was fundamentally internationalist as was Shakespeare.

From billionaire insurance executive **AMERICAN INTERNATIONAL GROUP CEO MAURICE "HANK" GREENBERG**—chairman of the trustee development committee at the Center for Strategic & International Studies while I was vice president for development—a promise to take the lead of the Center's expansive new development program. He invited me into his office and offered a chair before an arc of computers on his desk and showed me how he monitored the operations of his subsidiaries across the world. AIG was the world's largest insurance company and he was our most generous supporter.

From **ZULU CHIEFTAIN MANGOSUTHU BUTHELEZI**—President of the Inkatha Freedom Party, noted for his efforts for interracial reconciliation, and later the Minister of Homeland Affairs in Nelson Mandela's first South African government—fascinating insights about the racial conflicts still unresolved in the lead-up to Mandela's historic release from imprisonment, shared in conversations before receiving an honorary degree from The University of Tampa where I served as president.

From **AMBASSADOR TO THE UNITED KINGDOM ANNE ARMSTRONG**—chair of the CSIS board of trustees and also chair of the President's Foreign Intelligence Advisory Board at the White House—a check for $100,000 from a corporate donor that she handed me during a CSIS board meeting in Washington where she was formerly introducing our development plan for which I was staff officer. She was all business in diplomacy, industry and defense policy research, and this was no exception.

From **FEDERAL RESERVE CHAIRMAN PAUL VOLCKER,** later chairman of President Obama's Economic Recovery Advisory Board— who had accepted the chairmanship of the CSIS Advisory Board, which was another of my staff responsibilities—an economist's view of the critical relationship between the perception of credit and the assignment of value in the making of investment decisions by financial and political leaders. He was methodical, patient and unrelenting in his questioning of the briefing points.

From **FLORIDA GOVERNOR BOB GRAHAM**— later U.S. Senator and chairman of its Select Committee on Intelligence when the 9-11 terror attacks occurred and continuing on through the lead-up to the Iraq War while I was at UT and a member of his Florida Council of 100—a focused concern for the relationship of education and enterprise at all levels and in all sectors, always with an unfailing memory for personal names of guests arriving at his home or office, as well as his hosts on the road.

From **ACADEMY AWARD-WINNING ACTOR JOSE FERRER**— famous for his portrayal of Cyrano de Bergerac, who chaired the actor's committee of the Shakespeare Globe Centre's board of trustees while I was executive director—a high energy, message of support for the importance of theater in the life of the world and a tireless willingness to do whatever it takes to serve the cause, always with vision and genuine friendship.

From **ASTRONAUT SALLY RIDE**—the youngest astronaut, first female, and only LGBT person in space, who trained as an optical physicist, served as a university professor, and who was a participant in the CSIS strategic space program while I was its development advisor—a gift for making sense of complicated planetary systems effecting the exploration of space and the future of life on Mother Earth, and who, with a broad smile and firm handshake, was a soft spoken and often underestimated leader from whom we learned a great deal.

From **EDWARD TELLER, FATHER OF THE HYDROGEN BOMB**—both brilliant and outspoken as a nuclear physicist and natural philosopher, both friend and opponent of Einstein, Hungarian immigrant and long-time director of the Lawrence Livermore National Laboratory, with whom I visited before his address at UT, and on a bus ride to Cape Kennedy afterward—his unusual perspectives on science and politics affecting war and peace which led me to thoughts of rocket science and robust leadership as crude partners, at best.

From **KING OF CALYPSO HARRY BELAFONTE**—a confidante of Martin Luther King, Jr. who was more than a popular entertainer, but also a tireless advocate for the rights of people as citizens— his old office was across West 57th Street from Carnegie Hall in New York City which became my office when I accepted responsibility for Shakespeare Globe's operations.

From **"TO TELL THE TRUTH" TV GAME SHOW STAR KITTY CARLISLE**—who was chair of the New York State Council of the Arts, awarded the National Medal of the Arts, and inducted into the American Theater Hall of Fame— to Shakespeare Globe supporters at a luncheon I hosted for her, the direct linkage of classical plays with civilized culture, with special emphasis of course on the role of The Bard.

From **CIA DIRECTOR JIM WOOLSEY**—who was legal counsel to our CSIS executive team —constant warnings about the clear and present danger of America's enemies which his recent remarks about the notorious leaker of American intelligence, Edward Snowden, epitomized: "I'd prefer to see him hang by the neck until he is dead, rather than merely executed." Treason to one's country is serious business, though it was never part of official discussion while I was there.

From **CANADIAN NOVELIST AND POET MARGARET ATWOOD**—winner of the Booker Prize for best novel in the English language published in the United Kingdom and the Arthur C. Clarke Award for best Science Fiction, a charming presentation of prose and poetry to an enraptured University of Tampa audience unused to hearing such soaring words, and our special guest at a reception afterward for adoring fans of her work in writing, teaching and advocacy.

From **PRIME MINISTER HAROLD WILSON OF THE UNITED KINGDOM**— head of government and leader of the Labour Party— emphasis on opportunity through education allied with the aim of taking better advantage of rapid scientific progress, during Commencement Exercises at UT in his formal address and private conversation.

To

Bobbie

Published by:
Hamilton House Publications, LLC
Post Office Box 89
Hamilton, New York 13346
www.tokeepusfree.com

ISBN-13: 978-1530480272
ISBN-10: 1530480272
BISAC: Political Science / General

TABLE OF CONTENTS

INTRODUCTION

Is no one in America safe? We are born free. But we cannot be safe unless we are free to fight for it. That is what keeps us safe.

"No one is safe in America" was the conclusion of a 68-year old grandmother in Nashville, Tennessee, Linda McFadyen-Ketchum, reacting to the recent mass shootings in San Bernadino, California.[1] This is true—no one can be totally safe. It is also true that everyone is born free. Which is more important?

"I despise having to plan an exit strategy for myself every time I go anywhere, but I do," McFadyen-Ketchum continued. "I want to be ready to run when I hear the first shot. Some might call me 'hyper-sensitized,' but I call myself prepared and realistic. No one is safe in America."

For America, a nation on alert against domestic and foreign terror, that fear is on the minds of many people today. I grew up during World War II in Hempstead, New York on Long Island, near Mitchel Air Force Base which had a prisoner-of-war camp next door. I remember three fatal pilot training crashes in the village. We had regular air raid training drills when families took shelter in their basements. My grandmother ran a boarding house a few blocks away for "fly boys" allowed to live off base. We were not afraid. We lived to fight back.

On September 8, 1974 my brother was killed by a Palestinian terrorist bomb while co-piloting a TWA flight from Tel Aviv to New York in which all 88 aboard were lost. We were angry and never forgot it. Decades later, I was asked to help organize a campaign to secure American friends for the "Arab University of Jerusalem." In honor of my brother's loss I agreed, because I saw it as part of a fight for freedom by the Palestinian people to rid themselves of oppression.

A mighty quest for freedom is America's exit strategy to overcome the fear of domestic and foreign terror that dominates the news today. When America declared the "War of Independence" in 1776, Americans fought to free themselves from the autocracy of King George. When Americans adopted the first written constitution in the history of the world in 1789, its first words, stated in the Preamble, were for what was to become a democracy of freedom. When Americans fought the Civil War, it was a victory for freedom from slavery in 1865. When, in 1991, the Soviet Union succumbed in the ending of the Cold War, it was a victory for America and the free world.

Our mandate all along has been to keep us free. We cannot be safe unless we are first free to fight for it, and that base of freedom is what keeps us safe. When Francis Scott Key wrote of America as "the land of the free and the home of the brave," he was linking the courage to fight with the cause of freedom. That is what we must do. To keep us free is only possible when we are brave. When we then turn to our safety, we will be turning to it with all our strength at the ready. To be free of unfreedom is the first and ultimate step of being safe from unsafety.

The daily headlines shout that America and the world are caught in an interminably dangerous threat of terrorism. But, terrorism is not an interminable danger. We are the land of the free because we are brave. America will overcome terrorism by waging the same relentlessness fight for the way of freedom that we fought to win the War of Independence. But this can happen only if we live as a "land of the free and home of the brave."

The Preamble is the introduction. By going to the Preamble of the U.S. Constitution, we are going to the first fact of the law of the land and the heart of our nation. This is where we will find our national purpose and America's DNA. It helps us understand that we are not in a war of civilizations so much as we are in a fight for civility itself. The fight really begins with the Preamble's mandate "to secure the Blessings of Liberty, to ourselves and our Posterity." This is the message we honor in the Constitution:

"We the People of the United States, in Order to form a more perfect Union, establish Justice, insure domestic Tranquility,

provide for the common defence, promote the general Welfare, and secure the Blessings of Liberty, to ourselves and our Posterity, do ordain and establish this Constitution for the United States of America."

The Preamble is the singularity of civil law for America as a free country, and it opens the way out of the world meta crisis which besets us. The meta force that counters it, when released, is our freedom—the heart of America. Its simplicity stands at the center of perhaps the greatest complexity we have ever seen—global terrorism in both its causes and its consequences.

The Preamble is the nucleus of our solidarity as a people that converts the drive of our national soul into the acceleration of our national security. It is the drive, the nucleus, and the acceleration of America's long game in which every play counts every day.

That one sentence crafted by our forefathers is the creative gene which aligns our own DNA with the organizing DNA, or ODNA of our nation. It has been and is the law and order for what we do and how we do it.

The singularity of freedom speaks of human rights and responsibilities. The Preamble is the moral and legal authority of the American government—it should be the first plank of both political party platforms. And it needs to be the number one commitment of every candidate for office, starting with each of the presidential candidates in the 2016 election season.

But there is a problem here. While the Preamble is considered to be the Constitution's introduction, the Articles and Amendments which follow are, for practical purposes, considered to be the Constitution itself. That is a view too often expressed and essentially why the Preamble, though a set of sacred principles as some have called them,[2] is not a primary reference either in the law itself or the purpose to which it is applied. That ongoing mistake has led to heart failure in our body politic.

Freedom, as expressly proclaimed in the Constitution, is the essence of the oath taken by every elected official. They are all called to create and sustain that freedom as the moral equivalent of a war that would otherwise lead to the loss of precious lives and fortunes. As human beings living in a civilized society, we are obligated to keep one another free in order to be safe so we may lead our lives in a livable world. But how can we do that if we suffer from untreated heart failure?

I. FIRST FACT

Should we be honoring the Constitution in our political platforms? The Preamble is our first fact of law.

The body politic of America has taken a wrong turn. Some say it may be too late to turn it around, too late to return to the basic values that enabled the United States to become leader of the free world, too late to continue as the most prosperous nation in history. I don't think so.

I've served as a teacher of history and leadership—a former college president, administrator and professor—who is alarmed by the urgency of the need to overcome America's political dysfunction reflected by the fact that most Americans essentially overlook it by not voting. I believe that we must hit our collective pause button, return to our national soul and regain our national solidarity in order to recharge our national security. And I have come to believe that we can do that right now.

Counterterrorism and counterinsurgency are vital and necessary to keep us safe. However, keeping us safe is not our goal as a nation. It is a strategy to help us achieve our greatest goal—to be free.

The anger and frustration of so many with the way that federal and state governments function is understandable. Yet, most everyone has forgotten our national purpose that is stated in the first sentence of the law of the land: known as the Preamble of the United States Constitution. To honor the Constitution and to remind us that all other issues ought to be seen in its light, this statement—the heart of our nation—should be the first plank in the political platforms of both parties:

"We the People of the United States, in Order to form a more perfect Union, establish Justice, insure domestic Tranquility, provide for the common defence, promote the general Welfare, and

secure the Blessings of Liberty, to ourselves and our Posterity, do ordain and establish this Constitution for the United States of America."

Both parties should endorse this Preamble as their first cause in the first clause of their national platforms, immediately. This leading sentence of the law, with all it "ennobling language," according to the legal historian and University of Georgia Distinguished Research Professor Peter Charles Hoffer, "was presented to the Convention at the eleventh hour and accepted without a murmur by the delegates" of the Continental Congress at its 1787 Constitutional Convention in Philadelphia.[1]

As the founders saw it, the prime task was to keep us free. Americans fought valiantly to win their freedom and to pass it on to their posterity. The task was not primarily to keep us safe. If that had been true, we'd not have fought for our freedom. We'd have run for our lives, but that's not what we did.

Some Americans, actually, are more afraid of losing what they have, from real or imagined threats, rather than fighting for their freedom, which is what they need to keep what they have. What they miss is that in order to win, we must first create a "new birth of freedom," as President Lincoln is famously remembered for saying in his Gettysburg Address of 1863.

The Preamble of the Constitution makes plain the doctrine of freedom to which Lincoln referred. He knew that. It is our cause, where the answer to our anger begins. It is why, above all, we must honor the true Constitution before all.

Our political commitment to that should be on the public record, with the Preamble set forth word for word, explaining what it is and what it means to party members and all the citizens of this country who pledge their allegiance to the nation as they honor our flag. We should waste no time on more empty talk.

Going on the record will supply what frightened people, insecure politicians, and a captivated press are missing, which is the truth about what's actually going on. We the People are actually living of the news, by the news, and for the news. Many others, who are preoccupied with more pressing personal issues ignore the news and awaken later to news they don't like. Knowledge usually beats ignorance.

The Preamble speaks to the basic truth that sets us free and keeps us free. It's the soul that leads us to our solidarity as a people and our security as a nation. This happens only, however, if we live it together and with our friends in other nations. The political, economic and cultural benefits are obvious.

- The Preamble is America's statement of national purpose.
- It's the soul of our freedom, the seat of law and order, the source of the American Dream and our DNA as a nation;
- It's the ticket to nonpartisanship, to policy-centric leadership;
- It's the deflator of the ballooning alienation that threatens to blow up our political system while trying to cure it.

Understanding the Preamble and following its mandates is our most direct way out of the unprecedented political difficulties we face as a nation. This is not a partisan conservative or liberal issue. It is an American issue. I believe this is what history teaches us and what leadership requires of us. But our basic rights and privileges, as envisioned by the founders, have been hijacked by special interests in the public forums of government, and are being held hostage by the allures of upward mobility in which self-serving opportunists are caught up. These opportunists have stepped into the vacuum created by the public's abdication of its responsibility for paying attention. Indifference can kill.

I believe we can count on the Preamble to play a critical role in leading us to the new birth of freedom of which Lincoln spoke. For that to happen, we must make it part of our national agenda as well as our personal agendas as citizens of this nation. And we should make that happen immediately, as those who aspire to be our leaders sit down to shape their proposals for their platforms.

After all, it is the truth that makes us free—free from the slavery of domination by any one. We put our faith in this truth, do we not? We dedicate ourselves to it. Our lives become purposeful as never before. And that leads to the joy of certain pursuits in an uncertain world. Scripture has told us so. Scholars have done the same.

We may disagree about what that truth actually is, but we can agree on the values behind our search for truth in the changing times and circumstances we have. The Preamble is the truth, because it contains the values that are the basis of all political platforms — not only those of the opposing parties, those of the candidates, and those who serve in the seats of power in the Congress, the Presidency, and the Supreme Court.

We've learned that freedom of conscience is the vessel which holds the core combination to truth—faith, thought, and expression. When enjoyed by the people, these three concepts together set us free. Altogether, they empower our rights as they simultaneously encumber our responsibilities.

It is only logical, therefore, that we consider the Preamble to be the political platform we study, adopt and live by. Yet, today, almost no one is talking about these basic principles which embody our values. And those who are, bless their hearts, are just tipping their hats.

When we follow it, our history and our leadership teach us that the Preamble is the highway to freedom for all Americans. As it becomes the leading light for the law of our land, it is also a light for the world. To achieve this result, we must orient all relevant aspects of our learning toward its meaning and direction. As this is achieved, we will realize the advantages that flow from it.

I am a believer in servant leadership—leadership which places service to others before service to self. It is the opposite of fervent follower-ship in which service to self comes first. Servant leaders think for themselves *about* others. Fervent followers think about themselves *before* others. Servant leadership saves our souls. Fervent follower-ship destroys them.

16

To conserve our values, we must liberate our energy as a nation. To keep what we value most, we must be free to pursue it with all the energy we have. To do that, we must stick to our promise as a nation. Our promise is freedom.

This is America's DNA. The essence of this DNA is based on conserving values, liberating energy and keeping the freedom. That is what the seed of our soul does. The law and the order that follows grows from that seed. The promise of freedom is America's purpose. It is clearly stated in the Preamble of the Constitution, the leading sentence of the law. As we follow that lead, we will be more purposeful and productive as a nation. And we will be a more creative force in the world. This is the basis of our solidarity.

When James Madison and company declared: "We the People," they thought that the Constitution "would have not only the force of law but the force of a moral power far greater than that of kings, prelates and tribal rulers combined."[2] This is our security—the moral authority that overcomes fear and overturns kings. This elevates the Preamble as the genesis of America's civic religion. And, despite our not infrequently erratic ways, our official attitude is akin to worship. Alexander Hamilton added that "No legislative act contrary to the Constitution can be valid. To deny this, would be to affirm that the deputy is greater than his principal; that the servant is above his master; that the representatives of the people are superior to the people themselves."[3]

With our eyes on the prize—"We the People"—we will experience a growing capacity to lead ourselves, and this will enable us to lead others from greater strength of character. That's the thesis. The world will change because leaders everywhere will notice, and they will follow freedom and creativity as they see it, each in their own way. The mutuality that emerges then becomes our joint security.

Our founders chose freedom because they believed in the idea of a free country in a free world. This is how they thought America could bend the arc of history. And this is what America has done — when it has worked at its best.

"Nation building is in America's DNA. It dates back to the days of the Revolution when the founding fathers invented the concept of popular sovereignty—the idea that you cannot have a national government without a collective will. The framers of the Constitution fervently hoped that this concept would become contagious, spreading around the world and thus ensuring America's security."[4] This is a good summation of Jeremi Suri's argument about America's outlook from the time of George Washington to that of Barack Obama: from seed to solidarity to security so to speak. This is why the meaning of America's DNA is "to keep us free," free from domination and free as people.

In his recent visit in America, Pope Francis addressed Congress at the invitation of Speaker of the House, John Boehner of Ohio. "I am most grateful," the Pope said, "to address this Joint Session of Congress in the land of the free and the home of the brave." A great ovation swept the hall, with broad smiles from both sides of the aisle. He went on to say that: "You are called to defend and to preserve the dignity of your fellow citizens in the tireless and demanding pursuit of the common good, for this is the chief aim of American politics."[5] *To keep us free.*

The Pope is well known for being compassionate. His message is a promise that people are to be empowered so that they may exercise their right to be free. "A political society endures," he said, "when it seeks, as a vocation, to satisfy common needs by stimulating the growth of all its members, especially those in situations of greater vulnerability or risk." He referred to "the many thousands of men and women who strive each day to do an honest day's work…to build a better life for their families…in their own quiet way sustain the life of society…and create organizations which offer a helping hand to those most in need."

In a word, the Pope seemed to be saying, people are freed to be what we Americans would call producers. This is what makes a nation viable and strong. This is what can lead to solidarity and security that is steadfast against whatever headwinds may be blowing and from wherever they may come. Our soft cultural power can transcend our hard military power and facilitate our mediating economic power. The U.S. Constitution is the official guide of American law. Its Preamble should lead the daily playbook of American citizens. Whatever the nature of our political views, we should honor it.

Professor Hoffer observes that the Constitutional Convention "created a formula for American constitutionalism that has weathered over two hundred years of partisan contest." He said, further, that: "the Preamble is a series of positive commands to the government to perform its duties in the best interest of the people."[6]

He then goes on to point out that George Washington, in his 1796 Farewell Address, warned: "All obstruction to the execution of the laws, all combinations and associations, under whatever plausible character, with the real design to direct, control, counteract, or awe the regular deliberation and action of the constituted authorities, are destructive of this fundamental principle, and of fatal tendency."[7]

II. FREE COUNTRY

Did the 9-11 shock shake the freedom meta force? Yes it did. It's still there, but still shaky. It needs to stop, sit still, and stand up.

America's freedom force was reawakened on September 11, 2001. This freedom force is America's meta force, the force that runs through—yet transcends—all other forces in our system of government. The meta force is not a super force of commanding influence. That doesn't exist. Rather, it is a pervasive force of persuasive influence. Not top to bottom.   But center to circumference. Command and control is urgently necessary in times of emergency. But it always gives way, as it must, to collaboration and consent in order for people to be fully responsive in a free world.

Terrorists struck their targets at the World Trade Center and the Pentagon, before they were interrupted over a Pennsylvania cornfield on their way to the Capitol in Washington. The government and the country were asleep at the switch, unaware and unprepared for looming danger. We awakened in shock and awe. In the immediate aftermath, we were jerked to attention. The state of America changed abruptly. We searched our souls. What had happened? We weren't sure what to do. Let alone how we should go about doing it.

My wife Bobbie and I were sitting on a plane at Los Angeles International Airport awaiting takeoff. After an extended delay, we were ushered back to the gate's waiting area. As we deplaned and reentered the area, crowds were gathered around TV screens as someone cried out: "we've been attacked!" Our attention was diverted to see what was happening, and our thoughts immediately turned from astonishment, to sympathy, to concern, like everyone else's.

Then, the flashbacks began. It was September 8, 1974, twenty seven years ago almost to the day. My dad called saying my brother Jon's plane was down at sea off Greece and to pray for him as they were searching for survivors. TWA 841, had originated in Tel Aviv, with a stopover in Athens, on its way to Rome, and then to JFK New York. Jon was a former U.S. Air Force captain who was co-piloting the TWA flight with 88 aboard. As we learned hours later, the plane was lost with all on board.[1]

The cause for the loss was unknown at the time, though a Palestinian terrorist group claimed credit for a bombing, which TWA denied and the press subsequently ignored. The bombing was then confirmed early the next year. But it wasn't until years later, after the FBI had dropped the case, that the bomb maker was coincidentally found, belatedly brought to the US to stand trial, but then released after a judicial deadlock that happened over the futile objection of the FBI agent who had taken charge and who knew better. That bomb tracker was agent Mike Finnegan. He has since reported publicly about the details he found, and then privately to a gathering of our family on the 40th anniversary of our loss. [2]

But that wasn't all of the coincidences. Bobbie and I had, amazingly, lived near all the contact points related to the 9-11 crashes: in a Greenwich Village neighborhood of New York City close by the World Trade Center site; in Washington, D.C. across the river from the Pentagon; in Carlisle, Pennsylvania down the turnpike from the Shanksville cornfield; and in Tampa, Florida across the bay from the Bradenton flight training center where the hijackers learned to fly the jets. We were in wonderment about the coincidences.

After a time of mourning had abated and worldwide commiserations had begun fading, vengeful emotions stirred more widely, and talk of American retaliation bubbled to the surface. It became topic one in public conversation. So, the perpetrators were al Qaeda terrorists? Osama bin Laden was their leader? Where were they? Afghanistan? With weapons of mass destruction? What about Sadam Hussein next door in Iraq? Wasn't he implicated? Hadn't we better go after these bad guys and get them before they could do us more damage?

So, we went to war against "terror". First Afghanistan, then Iraq. Announcements of public alert levels at American airports became a daily phenomenon. Blaring television alerts became a regular morning disruption. An atmosphere of fear spread from Washington DC. We fought, stalled, regrouped, and pulled out. As a nation, we were exhausted. And now, years later, Iraq is divided and we are still undecided.

Our hard power had inflicted harm on the enemy, but had not done him in. Many thousands of lost lives, trillions of lost dollars, and countless degrees of doubt and disruption later, we began turning to the soft power of economic and political diplomacy. With some success and more frustration. Now, after the terror in Paris, talk about retaliation is back in the national headlines. This time it is about getting the next generation of anti-American bad guys, who are resentful of our leading role in a world they hate, who are threatening our friends, killing innocents, and wreaking havoc in the Middle East and beyond.

And shortly after that, with news of the mass shootings in San Bernadino, domestic terrorism has struck fear in the hearts of many Americans. President Obama followed with a prime time address from the Oval Office saying "Freedom is more powerful than fear." Yes, if that freedom is called out. We need to do that now, not only from the Oval Office, but also from Capitol Hill.

The last military commander to serve as President of the United States was Dwight Eisenhower, 1953-61. "Ike," as he was known, was the Supreme Allied Commander in Europe when D-Day was planned and launched. He was President of Columbia University before he became a candidate for President of the United States. Eight years later, in his Farewell Address, he began by saying:

> *"We now stand ten years past the midpoint of a century that has witnessed four major wars among great nations. Three of them involved our own country. Despite these holocausts America is today the strongest, the most influential and most productive nation in the world. Understandably proud of this pre-eminence we yet realize that America's leadership and prestige depends, not merely upon on our unmatched material progress, riches and military strength, but on how we use our*

power in the interests of world peace and human betterment."

Throughout America's adventure in free government, our basic purposes have been to keep the peace; to foster progress in human achievement, and to enhance liberty, dignity and integrity among people and among nations. To strive for less would be unworthy of a free and religious people. Any failure traceable to arrogance or our lack of comprehension or readiness to sacrifice would inflict upon us grievous hurt both at home and abroad."[3]

Is America's mission of freedom over tyranny, our leading power since independence, now reawakening to the new, post 9-11 day? Is it a meta force strong enough to counter the villainy of terrorism that hasn't gone away? That is a very relevant question, isn't it, as we enter another season of American presidential politicking? At its best, the historic mission of freedom has been the mantle in which the American psyche has been wrapped —officially since 1776 — but actually since the colonists first arrived. Isn't the claim that America is the greatest country in the world based on our claim of success as a free country that has risen to be the leader of the free world?

"The central idea upon which this country had been founded: that all souls—not just white male citizens of the United States of America—were entitled to personhood, dignity, and respect for their fellow men." This was Abraham Lincoln's belief in freeing the slaves, as Huffington Post Editor Howard Fineman saw it.[4]

By 2001, the mantle of freedom had worn thin. After 9-11 leaders began talking about their greatest responsibility being "to keep us safe." We certainly want and need to be safe. So far, there has been no sequel to that attack. But, it is seriously off point and misleading to claim that this justifies relegating the general responsibility for freedom to one of its specific responsibilities which is safety. Safe in relation to what?

There are many responsibilities to be considered in America's march for freedom—in the Preamble we see ten of them: "People," "Union," "Justice," "Tranquility," "defence," "Welfare," "Liberty," Posterity," Constitution," and "America." All of these responsibilities are to be pursued in balance as part of a particular national strategy in place at any moment in time.

Only a national freedom strategy can keep America safe and sustain it over time. Keeping us safe isn't the first responsibility of leadership. Whether intended or not, that claim amounts to fear mongering. That is so because it starts with what we *don't* want to lose, instead of what we *do* want to keep. For every American, what we do want to keep is our freedom.

To "keep us safe" emphasizes the threat and stirs withdrawal, instead of stressing the opportunity and stirring action to take care of our everyday lives and defend our right to do so. If we want to correct something we don't avoid taking action. Because, then, someone else steps into the vacuum and does it for us. Who, then would that be? The government? What does that do for our freedom to act if we stand by and let the government take over? Is a reminder about keeping us safe something we associate with small government or, actually, a summons to have a big government under the cover of fear? That would benefit whom?

The message we ought to be hearing is "keep us free!" We ought to be listening to how that requires service and sacrifice in order to secure peace with freedom. We should be talking about how to win freedom by helping to create equality among the people. We should not be talking about how to lose freedom by helping to create inequality among the people. The first is about winning peace. The second is about winning war. Which of these does the Constitution's Preamble consider our highest calling? Is its call "to keep us free?" Or is its call "to keep us safe?"

Freedom has evolved, in essence, as a mixed meta force. First, it seems to be everywhere. Then it seems to be nowhere. We argue about it. We think we know what it is, although it often means different things to different people. We don't seem to understand very well how freedom actually works. If we look at what is done in its name, our conduct suggests that our understanding of freedom is less than comprehensible. Still, the idea of freedom for America is most powerful. Freedom is our national purpose and a universal right of humankind.

Freedom has become more like a mixed metaphor, for something less than the meta force that it is when it is actually employed. Will we reclaim the mantle of freedom as the original, world-changing American idea? That is our challenge—and our opportunity.

Will this prioritization of freedom bespeak the greatness of America, or must we do armed battle with our enemies and win bloody wars against them in order to fly our flag atop the world? Can a nation reach the top and stay on top very long by brute force? Or, do we live in a world today where no nation can be the leader, at least in that way, for very long?

Leadership always comes from a center of influence. Wherever it may be reflected externally—from in front or behind or one side or the other—its creative energy radiates out from an inner core of shared values by a group. People gather round that center of gravity and attract others who help form a critical mass that produces a dynamic chain reaction and sustains the leading power for as long as the potential of its inner strength lasts.

True leadership is, therefore, a nuclear event. It is where our true strength lies. It is where America still is, despite the setbacks we have experienced. It is where Americans must reclaim who we actually are as a free people. It is also where, if we are to grow stronger as a liberating influence in our turbulent world, we must remember where we come from.

Conserving the values that drive our solidarity come first, because it is from them that we liberate the energy to secure our freedom from those who would otherwise do us harm.

Just after the Constitution's drafting had been finished, Ben Franklin was leaving the Federal building in Philadelphia when a lady came forward and asked him, "Well Doctor, what have we got, a republic or a monarchy?" He quickly replied "a republic if you can keep it."[5] Old Ben, at 81 years old, knew of which he spoke. Historians have called him "The First American" because of his extraordinary role in the struggle for America's independence and its early history as a nation. He was as worried about the struggles as he was encouraged by the progress through them. It would be tough going ahead.

That raises the question: can we keep it? Can we hold to the mission our founders set for us? Will we rise to its higher calling? Take it straight from the Preamble of the Constitution, we can succeed despite Dr. Franklin's worries about our ability to do so, while we take into account the swirling change of a world that never stops. Will we remember and respond?

When the Pope addressed Congress during his recent 2015 visit to the United States, he noted that "men and women of good will…shaped fundamental values which will endure forever in the spirit of the American people. A people with this spirit," he went on, "can live through many crises, tensions, and conflicts, while always finding the resources to move forward, and to do so with dignity. These men and women offer us a way of seeing and interpreting reality." [6]

This comment by the world's leading religious figure, known for his compassion, shows the wide influence and understanding that the Founder's vision and words and the application thereof have had over time and how they are seen by many leaders in the world today.

The Law of the Land in America is based in and on the Constitution, which is the heart of American law. And the Constitution is led by its Preamble—the soul, spirit and energy of our heart—our highest calling under the law. The purpose of the Preamble is to guide the leadership of the nation as it is empowered by "We the People." The philosophy which underlies the Preamble and its Constitution supplants the law of the jungle with a new set of dynamics as the Law of the Land.

By following these dynamics, a mainstream of laws and practices is created that saves us from the extremes of the lawlessness left behind. The Preamble is our genesis in law. It should be at the heart of our reputation domestically and internationally. So, as we begin our examination, let us consider where this may lead us.

We were led from the beginning toward a more energetic and efficient form of government, however imperfect it was, different from any other previously known. The founders of this experiment, a new way of empowering leaders and setting forth the law according to which the people would live, were dedicated to the idea of freedom from King George along with the freedom to run their own country.

They set the stage not only to free themselves but also their posterity. While doing so, the leaders among them imagined that they would be creating a model to consider for other nations, as well. The federalists of that time were supporters of the Constitution who "sought the stability and strength that could come from union, and from steady, effective government."[7]

This Constitution, then, as the Law of the Land led us away from the law of the jungle where it's might over right, away from the superiority of self interest and the implementation of frontier justice, and toward an experiment in republican government.

Too often, the doings of barbarity would defeat the beings of civility. This situation was to be rectified by a unique group of men who were leaders in this new land and who had studied carefully the thinking of scholars from around the world. They then created a document, led by the Preamble, that has become the basis for America's Law of the Land.

In a speech given at Stanford University in 1906, William James, who was the leading spokesman of American pragmatism—our gift of philosophy to the world—addressed the topic of a "moral equivalent of war."[8] He wanted to replace the belief in the necessity of war with a consideration of the duties of service to the nation. He may well have had the Preamble in mind because that would have been a succinct way of approaching the freedom and prosperity the founders were most concerned about.

Among the purposes of the Constitution's framers was the protection of American citizens against the scourge of war and the oppression that could result from a conqueror. The old Articles of Confederation,[9] that were designed to create a framework for a new nation, were failing. To better unite the various people who were parts of this experiment, and to create a sound basis for its future, the founders knew that preparedness was the best defense against the threat of tyranny. And the best defense is generally rooted in the law of the people rather than the rule of a club. The Preamble is a call for such future preparedness. The Articles and Amendments which make up this precious document have been and are the rock solid foundation that has kept us free.

Donald Trump, kicked off his presidential campaign for the 2016 Republican nomination for President with Neil Young's "Keep on Rockin' in the Free World." Although Trump has been appealing to the political right, the composer says he supports Bernie Sanders who is appealing to the political left. That says something big about America as a free country.[10] In politics, as in life itself, there really are two sides of every coin. That song holds a deeply pluralistic idea of what the "American Dream" is and can become. Written in 1988, it begins like this, with repeats of the "Keep on Rockin'" chorus:

"There's colors in the street
Red, white and blue
People shufflin' their feet
People sleepin' in their shoes
But there's a warnin' sign
on the road ahead
There's a lot of people sayin'
we'd be better off dead
Don't feel like Satan,
but I am to them
So I try to forget it,
any way I can.

28

I see a woman in the night
With a baby in her hand
Under an old street light
Near a garbage can
Now she puts the kid away,
and she's gone to get a hit
She hates her life,
and what she's done to it
There's one more kid
that will never go to school
Never get to fall in love,
Never get to be cool.

And surrounded by repeats of the chorus, it ends like this:

"We got a thousand points of light
For the homeless man
We got a kinder, gentler,
Machine gun hand
We got department stores
and toilet paper
Got styrofoam boxes
for the ozone layer
Got a man of the people,
says keep hope alive
Got fuel to burn,
got roads to drive.
Keep on rockin' in the free world"

The 800th anniversary of the "Magna Carta,"— the first charter of freedom—was celebrated in 2015. It is also the 150th anniversary of the 13th Amendment which freed the American slaves and also the 95th anniversary of "Women's Equal Rights" in America, when women got the right to vote. And it is, with perhaps too little fanfare, the 375th anniversary of a landmark "Freedom of Conscience" agreement, authored by the Reverend Roger Williams and the lay people of his Providence settlement. That document and its import was a precursor to the Declaration of Independence, the Constitution, and the Bill of Rights. It is good to pause and take note of this history and these moments and key documents that helped ground our future as a nation.[11]

In 1978, I was the new young president of The University of Tampa, Florida and had just formed a group of leaders to help map the institution's future, The New York Yankees were visiting the University, courtesy of team owner and former University trustee, George Steinbrenner. The Yankees at that time were World Champions, and I was a devoted, lifelong fan.

It was then that I met Yogi Berra, the late Yankee Hall of Famer. He was already a fabled storyteller often quoted for malapropisms. We exchanged pleasantries and he left me with a non-academic version of one of his famous lines. He told me, in any case, to remember that *"the future ain't what it used to be,"* and wished me good luck. Although I wasn't expecting anything in particular, I wasn't forgetting, because it was becoming more and more clear, that in creating a new culture at The University of Tampa, the future definitely would not be what it used to be. And it certainly hasn't been.[12]

Of course, the future never repeats itself, although sometimes it does seem so when things happen over and over again. There are too many changing complexities going on all the time. So, when a given situation faces us that seems like one that has occurred before, it is necessary to look at the lessons learned, to apply our basic principles and from that decide what should be America's response. That's the question which leads me back to the Constitution and to its Preamble, as the heart-of-the-heart of the Law of the Land.

Perhaps the toughest problem, in dealing with freedom, is considering how to balance it with its apparent opposite: equality. Free and equal are of course two different things. But they are not mutually exclusive. We can be free and equal at the same time. Indeed, we must be. Like right and left, they are complementary variables, both sides of an equation. We need them in some kind of balance so that one doesn't incapacitate the other.

After the battle of Gettysburg was over, President Abraham Lincoln began his famous address by noting that: *"Four score and seven years ago our fathers brought forth on this continent, a new nation, conceived in liberty, and dedicated to the proposition that all men are created equal."*[13] Shortly before the battle, Lincoln had issued the Emancipation Proclamation that freed the slaves held in the rebellious states of the Confederacy. He understood that liberty went with equality, and equality with liberty.

We the People, then, are responsible to keep from being trampled by overzealous proponents of one in disregard of the other. When that occurs, one takes over and the other is pushed out of the way. As responsibility narrows, irresponsibility arises, and the threat of violence increases. The action goes from hyperactivity to withdrawal. And the result can be explosive in the extreme, such as when loss of innocent life is the result. The Civil War is the most horrendous example in our history.

Freedom without responsibility risks the danger of tyranny. Those who give up responsibility leave the door open to those who are willing, even eager, to step into the vacated space and take over. In such a case, those who have relinquished their responsibility end up losing their rights. Participation in preserving freedom is a requirement for democracy to work.

It should be noted that abdication of responsibility can be either a matter of omission or commission. That is, by failing to stay informed, one can walk away from responsibility. The same is true if one fails to make his or her voice heard. That happens when one becomes convinced that what they do or say won't make any difference. Everything begins and ends with single individuals either acting or speaking who contribute to the energy level of what is happening. Democracy always rides on how that works out.

E pluribus unum was adopted as the national motto in 1782 by an act of Congress. It is Latin for "out of many, one." It referred to the confederated union formed from and by the separate states. This motto can now be found on the Great Seal of the United States carried in the beak of the bald eagle. This was the de facto motto of

31

the United States until 1956 when Congress adopted "*In God we trust*" as the official motto.

In recent years, we have come to reinterpret the meaning of *E pluribus unum* as "out of many peoples, races, religions, languages, and ancestries there has emerged a single people and nation—illustrating the concept of the melting pot." This is a metaphor depicting "a heterogeneous society becoming more homogeneous" emerging with a common culture, or perhaps described more artfully: "a mosaic in which different cultures mix."[14]

Whatever one's perception, the vision is that of a unity of people, living in a free society, governed by a representative democracy. This then further defines the meaning of freedom and the purpose of responsibility as the basis for creating and sustaining "equal justice under law," as the U.S. Supreme Court Building prominently proclaims on its facade. Promoting and supporting freedom and responsibility is the civic duty of "We the People," presumably our census population, and thus the test of our civic virtue as a nation. We should celebrate that wherever we can.

So, let us again visit the Gettysburg address and how President Lincoln summed up his charge for the future of the nation that would soon be staggering out of this terrible civil war. He said, after resolving that all those who gave their lives shall not have lived in vain: "that this nation, under God, shall have a new birth of freedom—and that government of the people, by the people, for the people shall not perish from the earth." This is certainly a message that resonates from that time to this day and is a guiding star for us to follow. Thus the path is laid out: from seed to solidarity and security.

How are we doing with following that path? Is freedom still the meta-force it could be if we gave it the respect it requires to work?

III. LEADING EDGE

Does freedom come before leadership? We can't lead if we aren't free to lead. And we aren't free to lead unless we know how.

Do we Americans understand freedom? Do we understand leadership? Does the free world understand either or both? Freedom feasts on leadership, but faces famine without it.

It is my conviction, after many years of being engaged with all aspects of leadership, both good and bad, that it requires freedom or it isn't possible. Yes, if you are hampered in your abilities or unable to think for yourself, then you cannot lead others or chart a direction for yourself. And those charged to be leaders can't do either effectively if they aren't well and able as whole persons in mind and body,

If we are to have the kind of leadership that will best serve the national purpose embedded in the Preamble, a compelling vision, along with the freedom to implement it, is required. Enabling freedom is that mission for America, and leadership requires strategies to overcome the inevitable obstacles before it. Is America regarded as the greatest nation in the world? Is that its reputation? Can it remain so? How important is that for the world to believe?

If there is one thing America needs to do really well—for its mission and vision and for its leadership and reputation in the world—it is creating and preserving freedom as its national purpose and preoccupation.

- This is the freedom that is expressed in democracy, justice, prosperity and peace. Is it not?
- This is the freedom that is reflected in rights and responsibilities. Is it not?
- This is the freedom that is applied to all its citizens. Is it not?

And this is the freedom seen by the whole world upon which our light shines and to which our linkages lead. Is that not so?

Freedom is the truth that sets us free to know more of the truth. We need, therefore, to live the truth in order to know the truth increasingly well and then to finally realize who we are as human beings; who we are as a country; and who we are as a world of people. Knowledge is something that cannot be taken away from us. Freedom is our great strength. Action is dependent upon both knowledge and freedom.

Freedom does not confer an urge to be managed. As we have become more dangerously addicted to power, we have become more resistant to being managed. Instead, we seem to be feeling a deeper need to be empowered. Power is really something that is enabled by leaders and accepted by those being led. It is not something that is managed and coerced. This power does not come from the barrel of a gun, but from the buoyancy of interchange among leaders and people. The authority of leaders who have power is earned by ideas and actions that are respected. This is enhanced by reputation, and especially by experience. Leaders are empowered by the feedback of the people.

The history of freedom in America can be traced to many founders. One of the most compelling, and perhaps least known yet most influential, was the founder of our smallest state, Roger Williams.[1] Williams was a London-born missionary who immigrated to America in order to minister to the Indians. He fell out with the Massachusetts Bay Puritans, and then founded the settlement of Providence in what is now Rhode Island. He reached a governing agreement with his followers in 1640 that was a historical first.

The agreement reached was based on a belief in what Williams called "freedom of conscience." This was a three dimensional insight that embraced freedom of religion, freedom of thought, and freedom of expression. These three seemed to encompass the concern for the soul, the mind, and the body. As he saw it, all were necessary for the freedom that comes from the discovery of truth. Seeking and finding truth is what sets one free. He believed that this was the root principle of humanity.

The truth is not something we simply create. The creation process involves converting the potential of energy that already exists into motion that is then released. However one perceives it, truth is there waiting to be discovered when we arrive on the scene and when the opportunity occurs. Our job is to free up our hearts and our minds and our souls so we may be able enough to perceive the truth that is around and within us. Finding that truth will set us free and enable us to find our way forward.

The U.S. Constitution is the first written constitution in the history of the world. It stands for freedom, starting with its Preamble. It charts the course for freedom for America, and by implication, for the world. Fear of any kind is the greatest threat to freedom, especially the fear of terror. I am thinking especially of the kind of terror inflicted on Americans who watched the planes rocket into the World Trade Center on television, as well as the few who did so in person.

What is important for people to see is that fear is like a bridge. Fear is a bridge before us, a bridge we need to cross, a bridge to the source of terror where that source is addressed, and a bridge where freedom overcomes that source of terror. This is not a matter of hope. It is a matter of courage. It is bravery in action.

Francis Scott Key got it right at Fort McHenry in 1814 when he extolled "the land of the free and the home of the brave."[2] Or, as our American Legion Commander in Hamilton, New York Ben Barrett told me: "the land of the free *because* of the brave." We are free because we are brave. No bravery, no freedom.

This bridge of fear is so near to us, it is never too far to cross. Yet we seem to be sleepwalking right by it. We should turn toward that bridge now, and begin crossing it—bringing along with us those for whom we care the most and who are inclined to join us. What will we have the moment we do that?

- We will have a Constitution authored *by* the people, *for* the people, with the authority *of* the people;

- We will realize that the court of public opinion is the people, and that the court of public opinion reflects our political will;
- And we will be reminded that, sooner or later, the opinion of the majority has the final call in American government.

The court of public opinion is the greatest weapon against the ghost of terror in the world. This is what historian Gordon Wood called the "vital principle" that underlies American government, society and culture.[3] That is because creating fear in the people, no matter whom they are, is what terror most needs to succeed and what it is least likely to get when freedom truly flourishes.

This is true because along with the creative energy of freedom comes equality. When we put them together, they create critical mass. That leads to chain reaction. And it does so at the velocity of light, which is their awareness. There is no stopping it, unless, of course, fear of terror once again intervenes. The more courageous we remain, however, the less likely that fear is to return. And the freer we are, the more courageous we'll be. This is embodied in the circle of life we are given.

Fear of terror[4] is the worst fear of the people, because it shuts down the freedom of action that enables a person to follow his or her conscience. That fear can be overcome by taking seriously the Preamble of Freedom as our guide to the American way of life. By law, we are called to be its witnesses. Are we ready and willing to be witnesses for that?

"Duty, honor, country"[5] must be more than a mindset of the nation's military, it needs to be the credo of all who are part of the national community. We are called to remember that the Preamble is intended to "secure the Blessings of Liberty." We need also to be reminded that freedom isn't guaranteed to last forever on its own. Freedom will be ours for as long as we understand it; for as long as we live it; for as long as we take responsibility for it; and for as long as we love it enough to teach it to our children.

A clear-eyed recognition of how freedom and terror may intersect in some form could lead us to a better understanding of how their multiple connections actually work. For example, if we assume that terror is the mirror image of freedom, then how would it look if the statement of freedom in the Preamble were reversed?

- Would "We the People of the United States" become "We the power brokers?"
- Would "in Order to form a more perfect Union" become "in order to form a house divided"?
- Would "establish Justice" become "institutionalize injustice"?
- Would "insure domestic Tranquility" become "instigate community disturbance"?
- Would "provide for the common defence" become "provide for world domination"?
- Would "promote the general Welfare" become "promote the rich but not the poor"?
- Would "secure the Blessings of Liberty" become "for only a few but not for all the many"?
- Would "to ourselves and our Posterity" be "for short-run fixes, not long-term solutions"?

Certainly, no president—or, for that matter, no pope—would condone dark answers to the assertions of light that illuminate the lamp of the Preamble. Following the light is not merely a matter of faith, but also a requirement of reason. Both are necessary for life to go on, are they not? Freedom, therefore, allows us to decide, whatever we do, what we follow and who we follow. Then we can be smart about what and who we don't.

Freedom is America's business, as we mind our own business, and as we make it our business to be aware of the nation's business. In business, we can go bankrupt if we don't have a good plan. In life, without a good plan we lose our freedom. The Preamble is the nucleus of America's business plan because it is the statement of our purpose, from originating mission to beckoning vision. That mission and that vision are the business of America because they are embodied in the purpose of our nation.

Freedom sets up leadership as a necessity, not just as an option. When people are free, they are able and obligated to choose. They have to choose if they are going to be free. The challenge is to make the right choices. By definition, free people must be persuaded to follow the path as laid out by those who framed our new birth of freedom. When it is working, leadership persuades. In fact, leadership embodies an agenda shared both by the leaders and by those who are led. In this reality, the led help to lead, and that's how the nucleus grows. That happens because followers turn into leaders, and as leaders listen to them, they turn into followers.

Those undertaking leadership responsibilities find that leading works more lastingly with the collaboration and consent of those being lead, rather than command and control. Just ask our most respected leaders.

- It pertains at all levels, from the macro-international to the micro-interpersonal;
- It ranges across the full scope of associations—from nations to neighborhoods;
- It applies to crises as well as to compromises;
- It resolves military battles as well as mutual aid agreements;
- It forms among people of all backgrounds;
- It works and is attractive to the attention span of anyone, anywhere, anytime.

So a reformer is not necessarily a special person trying to shake things up. Rather, a reformer can be anyone and everyone who is moved to change anything. That, then, is just about all of us. We become reformers because our physical and psychological makeup is constantly evolving and reforming, as does the world itself. Consider how we lead our lives as those who may be empowered and perhaps also as those who may be empowering others. What are ways that this is done?

- We take leadership roles with our families;
- We are involved with leadership in our businesses;
- We participate in the leadership of our government;
- We work with leadership in special interest groups;
- We lead our lives in changing times and circumstances.

Tom Peters came to speak at The University of Tampa soon after the publication of his groundbreaking best-seller, "In Search of Excellence."[6] He had the audience spellbound and in laughter. They were with him, it seemed, from start to finish. Afterward, when we had a little time together, he was adamant about the importance of getting people onto the action side of his equation. Tom was full of enthusiasm about releasing people's energy so they are motivated to want to get things done that everyone agrees are needed done.

Tom shared his concern that we are taught—what he called an "enumerative, rationalist approach" to thinking—that this way of thought dominates the management of our institutions and organizations. "The central problem of the rationalist view of organizing people," he said, "is that people are not very rational." But, he also said, "We like to think of ourselves as winners. So, there is no reason why we can't design systems that reinforce degrees of winning rather than degrees of losing."[7]

If we don't do that—create the kind of systems Tom was championing with a focus on degrees of winning—won't people become manipulated by fear, won't they become frustrated and angry enough and succumb to accepting shallow solutions that could lead to devastation and destruction?

- Think what happened in Germany before the rise of Hitler;
- Think what happened after Hitler took power;
- Think what happened in America with Hitler in power;[9]
- Think what America did to rebuild Europe after World War II.

What did it take for America and its allies to win that war? What did we as a nation learn from that experience? Have we used that learning to deal with new, yet similar problems, as well as the threats which created them? What could help us in these efforts? Did the Founders show us a path with guidelines to follow?

Are we looking forward to World War III?[9] If not, do we understand how modern technology has interwoven the world so closely—electronically and otherwise—that hair triggers in the Middle East can click an instant response in Middle America? When that happens, given the impact and scope of modern media, we sense an immediate fear and support immediate reaction in response.

How, then, will we respond when these situations occur? We have seen how "We the People" have responded in the past. How, then, can we use the wisdom of the Preamble to prepare ourselves and our leaders to keep us free while we, by our faithfulness to the Preamble, keep ourselves cool and more safe at the same time?

In the current system governing this nation, it can be said that there are all too many political puppets who will dance to the tune of otherwise good people who are behaving like semi-psychos in social bubbles.[10] And the rest of us are paying the price for our failure of vigilance.

Who are these people acting like that? Some are prominent politicians, some are prominent business or labor people, and some are prominent investors. All of them are pursuing their own interests at the risk of the public interest. Their mentality as regards public service is incomplete, to say the least, and the scope of their concerns is personally limited, to say the most.

Now, think about how we the people abandon our responsibilities. What percentage of us votes in elections? As many don't vote as do. Are "We the People" abandoning our responsibility for forming "a more perfect Union, establishing Justice, insuring domestic Tranquility, providing for the common defence, promoting the general Welfare, and securing the Blessings of Liberty, to ourselves and our Posterity?" Have "We the People" allowed the political process to fall into the hands of semi-psychos in social bubbles?

Writing about what he called the "post-capitalist society" in America, Dr. Peter Drucker exclaimed in disgust, "Elected representatives fleece their constituents to enrich special-interest groups and thereby to buy their votes. This is a denial of the concept of citizenship."[11] The Austrian-born management consultant was widely published and recognized with the presidential Medal of Freedom for his remarkably productive works of interest to both businesses and nonprofit organizations. Productivity was a central part of Drucker's core message for any organization, government included. The Preamble undeniably depends upon the productivity of the people.

Who, then, are these semi-psychos in social bubbles? They are people so caught up in themselves that they have lost touch with the larger political reality that is America. Their mind-sight has become politically shallow and purposively narrow. Semi-psychos in social bubbles are anywhere and everywhere we might look. They show little respect for those outside their social bubbles. They are self-absorbed. They are, in essence, control freaks. They are often people in positions where they exercise power over many others. They will, whether intentionally or unintentionally, take away your birthright of freedom while they feed your worst instincts.

They are those who regale us with a game plan that having our way at any cost is the mission. Their solution is set forth like this:

- Don't worry about the freedom part;
- Don't waste time trying to think things out;
- Suit up for battle and get with it;
- Let the bad guys know who's boss.

Take hold and charge ahead! That philosophy has gotten us into a lot of trouble. And when we haven't done that we are told it shows that we are weak. And we've got to be strong. Winning is what makes us strong, no matter what!

The message that we are given is that the world is going to hell in a hand basket because America hasn't stood up. We've got to fight if we want to "win." If that means going to war, then so be it. When we hear words that convey that message, whether literally or not, we are listening to psycho speech. Such psycho speech makers certainly come across as good persons which they may very well otherwise be. Beneath the surface, though, they are suffering dangerous delusions. They don't quite realize, at least in their psycho speech making, that freedom must be lived in all its respects if it is to be won in all it regards. Freedom is fancy if it doesn't last.

Consider the shooters who have killed unarmed citizens (and often turn their guns on themselves).[12] What was their state of mind when they pulled the trigger? What were they trying to accomplish? Could their extreme translations of "winning" be in any way comparable to the would-be leader who gets carried away in making outrageous statements to unsuspecting crowds that stoke their fears and edge them on to battle?

The tinder in the heightened blood pressure of those addressed then skyrockets to explosive levels waiting for a match to set it off. Does this sound like any of the loud voices offering their leadership for public office today?[13] If it does, run the other way. Entrapment to demagoguery pays no dividend.

So, what about the associations with which we the people are involved. Our associations all depend upon leadership, and live or die because of it. As Alexis de Tocqueville once said: "The science of association is the mother science. All else depends upon it."[14] Leadership emerges in the formation of associations of every kind in different formulations. Always has been. Always will be.

However, leadership often arises from a single source, is championed by a single voice —President of the United States? Voice of a private citizen? The champion and the message are at the center of like-minded people who are drawn together by a common purpose. Their solidarity increases as the power of the message reaches wider and deeper into the minds of others. Their mutuality shelters them from undue harm that might otherwise be inflicted upon them. So, what are the implications of this leadership for "We the People"?

If the adage we have been taught at home, in church and school is taken to heart, then "the truth will set you free."[15] What is the truth that we believe in, the truth that we think about, the truth that we express? In America, that truth would be the singular message of freedom with all its nuances of meaning. And that truth, whatever it is, always leads us. Does your truth do that for you? Do you have a grip on your own truth? Does America?

If we are to be a well-led association of peoples, such as the United States likes to believe it is, then the complexities of our politics must be overcome in order to deal with the difficulties we face as a republic that espouses democratic capitalism. Accomplishing this strength of society will continue to take the very best public leadership America has in order to look after those who are disadvantaged and disaffected by our leadership. I submit that the Preamble is our leading source of direction for doing that.

Those who are among the advantaged, who are our strongest assets, bear a great responsibility to use their freedom to serve the high ground for all humanity. We must set ideology aside. It must take a back seat to one's humanity. We are human first. We must proceed from that space and place. We are obliged to others for our very existence. Our future depends on us and them. It is "We the People" who keep ourselves free. When we are united, we are prepared to lead ourselves and others for a future in freedom.

IV. INVOLUNTARY SERVITUDE

Is unfreedom unAmerican? In America we believe in choosing freedom over servitude. But we have trouble acting like we do.

There is a duality that exists between freedom and unfreedom. How does this duality play out as the rest of the world looks at what they understand happens in America today? Are there elements of the truth about how we live and how we are led that can be interpreted and twisted for or against the interests of other nations? Perhaps what is not seen is that freedom and unfreedom can become codependent in an unhealthy way. Instead of being integrated parts of an organic body, they can become rigid parts of a dissolving corpse.

The ties that bind lie in the kindred souls of the people. The Pope can and does speak to this directly. His compassion leads the way. It can be transformative. People feel the difference. They are drawn to it. Why is this Pope so popular? He lives his compassion and it shows. Who are the leaders in America who follow this example? Are they heard and supported or, in the end, do they become victims of those spreading fear and irresponsibility?

Co-dependency has been defined as a "learned behavior that can be passed down from one generation to another. It is an emotional and behavioral condition that affects an individual's ability to have a healthy, mutually satisfying relationship. It is also known as 'relationship addiction' because people with codependency often form or maintain relationships that are one-sided, emotionally destructive and/or abusive."[1]

In such a situation, one person controls or manipulates another because of the other person's incapacity to act without help. When one incapacitates oneself by avoiding responsibility and giving up one's inherent rights, that person facilitates such co-dependency. This process may just as well apply to a group or to a nation.

What gets less attention than it should is the idea that this co-dependency can happen to self-interested groups of otherwise good people. Such groups get wrapped up in their own views of things just like individuals do. They come to believe that these disparate views should apply to everyone, and that their job is to make this happen.

Addicted to what is believed their vision means and to what it thinks must happen to accomplish it, these groups then seek to inflict their predilections on others who differ with them and who will be harmed by them.

Situations become even more difficult when a singular case of egomania happens to metastasize into hyper-social egomania in which members of a group begin feeding off each other's obsessing egos into a frenzied fixation on a perceived threat. All else equal, the universe narrows down its mutual concern to the exclusion of all else. Such an obsessive-compulsive mindset can deteriorate into the symptoms of disorder.

The tender-loving-care of one person lifts up another. But, when that TLC from the first person goes missing, the second person becomes more and more subject to the wishes of the first. What is striking is the degree to which we the people have now become codependent in a society in which the more powerful partners, those with the resources, dominate the less powerful.

The rich resist empowering the poor out of fear of losing their power as the rich. What may go unnoticed is that the rich can become dependent upon the poor. They need the poor to be kept poor and powerless so that they, the rich, can hold on to their power. In other words, as this occurs, the rich keep the poor down to keep themselves up, and then this dependency of the poor on the rich creates a dependency of the rich on the poor. The circle is complete and the beat goes on.

The healthy powerful then become dependent upon the unhealthy powerless to keep themselves in power. This self-perpetuating duality seems to be in the nature of freedom itself. The freedom of the most powerful can become dependent upon the unfreedom of the least powerful. So the most powerful become reluctant to give up their power to the least powerful because they need them to continue being without power.

And many of them follow this path while believing they are actually helping the others to change their ways and become more like them. Could this be true of some politicians and their constituents? Of financiers and their investors? Of manufacturers and their customers? Of service providers and their clients?

This co-dependency creates a mutual servitude between both the powerful and the powerless. This servitude then becomes involuntary with the loss of objective awareness about what is going on by each side. And then the fog of misfortune closes in on their minds, clamps down on their hearts, darkens their souls, and finally dissolves their bodies. They are then gone, no longer free people, but the walking dead, like political zombies we can laugh or cry about. Are we ourselves unknowingly among the zombies? Are we not yet into a responsible adult mode about our duties to "live free or die," as they like to say in New Hampshire?

Taken to its extreme, servitude makes objects out of subjects, aliens out of humans, creates hostility as the norm, and leads to savagery in the ultimate. A recent CBS television report showed how Patrick Desbois, a Catholic priest determined to expose the forgotten massacres by the Nazi death squads who murdered millions of Jews in World War II, had located and uncovered many dozens of their killing fields. And the Nazis were Germans whose great lineage was overcome by desperate circumstances.

Desbois saw that their genocide was a horrific display of a "human disease that sleeps and awakens from one generation to the next." Take ISIS as a current example. Like the Nazis, ISIS fighters believe their killings are justified. In a world connected by the Internet, we are all witnesses to such despicable conduct. It's not the same ideology, but underlying it—it's the same disease.[2]

I'll never forget when Frank Borman spoke years ago at a meeting in Miami that I was part of. Borman was the former astronaut tapped to head Eastern Airlines. He talked persuasively about how freedom can turn into slavery and how slavery can turn into freedom. The direction would always be up to us. We can let freedom go or we can lift it up. The same situation works regarding slavery. Do we have the grit to fight and work for freedom? Will we work to regain and retain what we worry about losing?

Borman once said: "Capitalism without bankruptcy is like Christianity without Hell."[3] He was chairman of Eastern Airlines when he said that, and that was when Eastern was running out of money. So, it wasn't surprising that he concluded "It's hard to see any good news in this." But there always seem to be two sides of every coin and every issue. The other side of freedom is unfreedom, sometimes known as slavery, a state that clearly means dependency and usually leads to destruction. Knowing that helps. Because it can keep us focused on where we want to go.

Lord Patrick Devlin of Britain notably wrote about how individuals deal with the bonds joining them in common morality to a society that can support them. He said: "Society is not something that is kept together physically; it is held by the invisible bonds of common thought. If the bonds were too far relaxed the members would drift apart. A common morality is part of the bondage. The bondage is part of the price of society; and humankind, which needs society, must pay its price."[4] We need to ask ourselves if we as a people are addicted to the unfreedom of involuntary servitude as circumstances suggest?

The Declaration of Independence, penned in large part by Thomas Jefferson, set forth certain accepted truths that have become a world-wide standard of human rights. The opening sentence of its second paragraph is the centerpiece: "We hold these truths to be self-evident, that all men are created equal, that they are endowed by their Creator with certain unalienable Rights, that among these are Life, Liberty and the pursuit of Happiness."

It should be noted that it is the *pursuit* of happiness that is set forth. The rich and those holding power use the pursuit as a carrot to be pursued by those who are dependent on them. Realizing the dream is always tomorrow, someday, in the future. And the freedom that realizes happiness is suppressed for a pro-forma involuntary servitude that has been created and is being perpetuated.

Have we become indifferent to this new reality in our lives? Have we, for example, became so intoxicated with the exhilaration of victory in the Cold War that we don't see it actually as the triumph of freedom over unfreedom? Do we see it simply as the defeat of Soviet power by American power? Do we see that it is values that drive power, and that the resulting power lifts up those values? Do we see that emotions actually organize thought? Do we see that the Preamble is the soul of America?

These are among the questions to be applied as we face the challenges of freedom in America, and of freedom in the rest of the world. How might our neighbors, our allies, those who oppose us, and those who are just struggling to survive look at America's leadership as they assess what they can see of our track record on the freedom front? The information revolution, we know, has dramatically expanded what is shared around the world instantly.

To be the recipients of the fruits from the seeds planted by the Preamble, we must overcome the meandering fears from all kinds of terror threats, and the resulting confusion flowing from our lingering worries about them. Where I live in Central New York, the Loomis Gang was "the largest family crime syndicate in 19th century America."[5] In the mid 1800s, it terrorized many of the small farms and villages of Madison, Oneida, Otsego and Chenango counties with thievery, horse stealing, barn burnings and other acts of physical violence. The raiders would then disappear into their rural retreat in "Nine Mile Swamp," beyond the reach of the law.

As the word spread from place-to-place, the fear of being terrorized, humiliated, and robbed was palpable. The law didn't stop it. But after nearly two decades of mayhem, family attrition and infighting, an angry mob finally did. This leads us to consider what do we have to go through before our culture of fear can be overcome by a true culture of freedom? Is an angry mob always the answer? Whether it's local in person or global in extension?

All our relationships arise somehow from interactions with someone, with one phenomenon or another. What actually are these relationships and what is behind them? Can we get a closer look?

Change happens not only because one person is particularly single-minded and strong, or brilliant and unselfish, but because others are attracted to an idea someone presents, and groups organize to make things happen. This occurs when ideas show promise of significantly improving the status quo of people paying attention.

Take, for example, the amplifying chorus of voices saying that inequality is a root cause of many other issues such as violence and crime, health and education, budget and debt, issues that must be addressed in a bipartisan way by politicians, the press and the public. Where do we start?

Mohandas Ghandi, who led the peasant protests that turned India from a colonial protectorate into a world power, once observed that "poverty is the worst violence."[6] We moderns associate poverty with the absence of money, not recognizing that the absence of money usually deprives one not only of adequate food, clothing, and shelter, but also leads to broken families, lesser relationships, poorer healthcare, and the loss of mindfulness that so often leads to worry, depression and anti-social activity.

All of this tends to deprive one of the helping supports associated with a healthy life. The totality of it all, as Ghandi himself had seen in South Africa and India, would do violence to general care and nurture, and therefore to one's soul. This, one might contemplate, could be the darkest form of terror one might face. Thus, the economic, psychological, and spiritual distress it produces foments anger, panic and turmoil.

So violence, poverty, and the fear of these ills, would seem to explain a substantial part of the tension that disrupts the peace and calm of pleasant living, the happiness of good living, and the strength of loving family and friends. Poverty often does violence to the ordinary soul and subsequently to the society surrounding it.

Duality—such as violence and non-violence, wealth and poverty or just plain weight and motion—was a basis of Albert Einstein's insight about the equivalence of energy (which is our strength), and matter (which is its realization). A world away from Ghandi, Einstein saw in the equivalence of energy and matter what he initially called a "theory of invariance"[7] and what we have come to know, quite differently, as the theory of relativity. This has practical, everyday relevance for us because relativity, in Einstein's work, referred to relationships. And relationships are what matter in all things great and small.

This is important for us to understand as we grapple with our everyday issues. Einstein first and foremost saw constancy in an unchanging set of relationships, not relativity in the form of changing relationships. Relativity implies a changing set of relationships such as in values, as if Einstein was saying "everything is relative." No, as an American immigrant fleeing the Nazis, he wasn't saying that. Einstein knew, indeed he proved, that there are standards of objectivity in relationships. He also knew about the freedom he later sought in America.

Einstein saw what were unchanging standards in a world we cannot escape, and upon which we depend. Relationships change constantly within that framework of time and space. He very much appreciated that and worked hard all his life to expand that point into a "grand unified theory" of the world. Unfortunately, he never found it, but the search continues. Will it ever end?

What we now know as the theory of relativity — as strange as it may seem—is actually akin to the old hymn "Rock of Ages."[8] Relativity, after all, is the rock that embraces the fundamental duality of energy and mass through the medium of light. Light is the constant—never changing in speed or direction. Energy is the potential—always present in one form or another. Mass is the matter—people always in motion. Energy produces matter, interacts with it, grows with it, and dies with it. Though the totality of available energy never changes, the mass does, depending upon the health of its system. So, we need to keep it healthy. This rock is our civil rock. Yes, I do believe there is a civil rock.

Right now, if we pause and take a deep breath, we can feel, and maybe even see in our mind's eye, a creative *drive* in the universe that people sense, find and follow. Part of that creative drive is the meta force of freedom. That drive gives them an idea of how the world works and leads them to join with others to form the makings of a nucleus of some kind.

The *nucleus* could be that of a family, a neighborhood, or a community, small or large. That nucleus, in turn, grows and *accelerates* with a commonly held vision which unites its followers and produces significant outcomes of an identifiable nature. That can occur gradually or, in our digital world, exponentially. It reflects the organizational DNA that is embodied in its nucleus.[9]

This organizational DNA or ODNA is like the genetic DNA from which individual people grow, and that is the fundamental basis of all living systems. The organizing DNA of **Drive, Nucleus and Acceleration** changes the world by uniting people in groups of common pursuit.

Not long ago, the Huffington Post's Howard Fineman spoke of the "DNA of American public life" while addressing the "enduring arguments that define and inspire our country."[10] ODNA contains the fundamentals of any functioning group of people. This message can lead us to a preamble of freedom, such as the one that exists in the first words of the U.S. Constitution:

"We the People of the United States, in Order to form a more perfect Union, establish Justice, insure domestic Tranquility, provide for the common defence, promote the general Welfare, and secure the Blessings of Liberty, to ourselves and our Posterity, do

ordain and establish this Constitution for the United States of America."

If the Preamble is to function well as the DNA of America, it must become the daily playbook not only of our leaders, but also of our citizens. And from our playbook, our scoreboard will be more easily read, understood, and followed.

The **Drive** of our DNA is its purpose—where we are coming from—the creative energy behind and within all that we do as citizens. This is captured in the opening words: *"We the People of the United States, in Order to form a more perfect Union."*

The **Nucleus** of our DNA is the mass which the drive creates. It reflects the way our citizens and our government operate. The operating principles are set forth in the following statements: *"establish Justice, insure domestic Tranquility, provide for the common defence, promote the general Welfare."*

The **Acceleration** of our DNA is the constant velocity of light which regulates its speed and direction. It is the vision of where we are going that gathers the means of our sustainability. As such, it would *"secure the Blessings of Liberty, to ourselves and our Posterity,"* and therefore, we *"do ordain and establish this Constitution for the United States of America."*

Altogether, this pre-ambulated DNA steadfastly sets out the organizational philosophy of America. The main text of the Constitution, the Bill of Rights, and the remaining Amendments, follow. The Congress, the President, and the Supreme Court are mandated to pay attention to what the words in these documents mean now, at this moment in America's time and space.

It is those in high offices, as the official leaders of the people, who are responsible for advancing what the founders wanted the new nation to produce. The Preamble spells that out. What does it mean now? Now—whatever we see, hear, think or remember—is all we have. We discover, then we rediscover, as times change. Is that not how the world works, how life is? A wonderful mentor of mine, Art

Frantzreb,[11] once responded with one word —"ego" — at a Washington D.C. lunch one day after I asked him what he thought is the greatest impediment to leadership. He was one of the pioneers of philanthropy in America, and knew that ego was also a great impetus for leadership. His point was about egoism overdone, at the expense of empathy. Leadership without empathy is not leadership. It is low-end management, without feelings for one's fellows.

Unfortunately, narrow interpretations of federal, state and local laws have now evolved as isolated islands that function like separated silos where segregated data lies on different platforms of thought. Each of them, in data-speak, has its own set of sensors that work in unique systems of unstandardized data. Each has its own metric profiles of contents. They don't speak the same language. They are without a common basis for analysis and understanding. What's missing, in such data-speak, is a common set of learning analytics, that is, tests and measures we can look at, talk about, and use. This is critical.

Roger and Hilja Wescott were among the dearest friends Bobbie and I have ever been blessed to have. He was valedictorian of his class at Princeton and a Rhodes Scholar, and she was valedictorian of their household and a roads scholar. We knew them during our years in Madison, New Jersey at Drew University. What a wonderful place that was. Roger *knew* so much about so much, and Hilja *felt* so much about so much. They had a widely devoted set of congenially mixed friends from college and community circles. What seemed to come out of their diversely assembled gatherings were experiences of learning and enjoying together. One would become part of an ambiance of caring, about all manner of subjects and relationships in story, song and laughter.

We miss them because that was such a time of fulfillment. We never thought about sharing a set of what we now call learning analytics, but we did share a subculture of experiential references that made dozens of us, at that time, an evolving social community. These communities are, sadly, not often found in many places today.

Without the breadth and depth of community experiences such as these—a way of living and sharing the life envisioned and fought for by our founders—how are we going to be comprehensive or strategic in our considerations of our future as a nation? How are we going to think of everything we should before we address tough situations? We need to know everything we can, weigh the information, make our choices, and then work out our plans.

With strategies such as we get with a plan in mind, we can go from problem to solution along chosen routes, through an evolving system of thought and action. Whatever the zigs and zags, a good strategy will help us get where we want to go. We can systematically follow a strategy that enables us to overcome conflicts along the way. It leads us toward a vision of where we want to be. It gives us confidence as we go. And we are more likely to get there.

Leo Botstein,[12] the forty-year president of Bard College, was a participant in a seminar I once led for new college presidents. His leadership at Bard and at the American Symphony Orchestra has been extraordinary. His secret may have come from the strict immigrant housekeeper of his childhood who had a saying that stuck with him: "All of life is organization," she would say. Allowing for the exaggeration and her motivation for being punctual about dinner, this is a point to take seriously. Botstein has overcome exceedingly difficult challenges. We must do so as well. But how? I suggest we start with the ODNA of our Preamble that is the basis of our make-up and heritage as Americans, and build our organized systems around it. In his own way, that is what Leo has been doing.

I am fascinated when I think back and note how often I've encountered references to the DNA of a group. The DNA of Disney, the happiest place on earth? The DNA of the Yankees, the winningest team in baseball? Harvard, the smartest university in the country? America, land of the free and home of the brave? We do not stop to examine the components of such images as these, let alone consider how true they may currently be.

Branding can be regarded in much the same way. Take, for example, my alma mater Colgate. Is it anything like the popular toothpaste with which it shares the same name?[13] Mind and mouth? Both do relate to the same family, actually. Both organizations work well, have good taste, look nice, and "don't forget to tell your friends." Branding is a shorthand term for labeling, most often for products. This is a handy mechanism. People react to impressions created for products as well as for ideas.

America's founders meant The Preamble to be a lot more than just the makings of an impression. They created an organized system, led by its mission and strategy, set out as a sequence of thought and word that would guide "We the People" with the spirit and substance of The Law of The Land. This would be the law and the order that enact and exact America's future.

But, unfortunately many do not see it that way. They have come to doubt a prosperous future. What, then, is a picture of the future that will earn our confidence and create a unified vision to bring us together to make that vision a reality? Is the current America a brand we wish to buy or in which we wish to invest?

V. SYSTEM CONFIDENCE

Are our politics dysfunctional? Yes. Our political system does not honor the Constitution's mandates in the Preamble.

America is an open society functioning within an organized system. No pope or president is likely to speak in these terms, per se, but they can hardly avoid thinking in them.[1] The terms are not mutually exclusive and, therefore, not implacable partners. They are, in fact, what knowledge and technology require to work productively for a people. Together, their cooperative functioning —as a society that prides itself on its openness and, which therefore, needs to be organized to be open— is essential for a sustainable future with freedom for America.

A system is a dynamic set of interconnected parts that form a more complex whole while performing a function. A society is an aggregate of people associated for a purpose, such as constituting a nation. Freedom is only free before we choose to exercise it. Then, of course, it has costs. Whatever and however each of us chooses, we make our choices in a larger society that functions as an interdependent system.[2]

Sensitive dependence on initial conditions, or what has been called the "butterfly effect," is the property of a dynamic system in which small change can produce large effects as the impact of its motion spreads. The butterfly effect[3] is a term applied to weather systems that was coined by Edward Lorenz at a 1972 conference of the American Association for the Advancement of Science in Washington D.C. when he spoke on the subject of "Predictability; Does the Flap of a Butterfly's wings in Brazil set off a Tornado in Texas?"

Because systems are affected by many influences, they are subject to relentless change. If they are closed systems, the changes will come from inside that system with a limited supply of energy which eventually is exhausted. If the system is open, change will come from both inside and outside the system and will have a greater capacity for energy regeneration. The open system, therefore, has a longer term potential than a closed system. The butterfly effect is more observable in an open system.

Weather systems are open systems. The butterfly effect obtains. America is an open society. Why wouldn't it apply to our political system as well? Wouldn't the viral effects spoken about in social media, such as in a YouTube video, then carried over worldwide television, be an example? Not only in America, but around the world? Why would China have such restrictions on Internet transmissions? Why would North Korea have an electronic blackout across its territory?

Five years ago a Tunisian street vendor, Mohamed Bouazizi, immolated himself after being forced off the street in Tunisia and set off the "Arab Spring" uprisings across the Middle East.[4] The after effects of that event are reverberating to this day. But the tinder box of emotions he represented was not happenstance.

In speaking about the functioning of systems—whether organized as corporations, agencies, unions, churches, communities or small businesses—Peter Senge thought they all, more or less, are what he called "learning organizations," with sub-cultures of their own. He observed that "the changes required will be not only 'in our organizations' but in ourselves as well."[5]

The central message of his landmark work: *The Fifth Discipline,* is that "our organizations work the way they work, ultimately, because of "how we think and how we interact." He said that "Only by changing how we think can we change deeply embedded policies and practices. Only by changing how we interact can shared visions, shared understandings, and new capacities for coordinated action be established." He then concluded, "we must redesign the internal structures of our mental models." And thus, we may imagine the founders envisioning the Preamble as the mental model of the American nation.

Do we have confidence in what the Preamble's mission of freedom might mean for America? Confidence matters because it reflects our strength of faith. And that supplies the energy for facing the future. The greater our spirit and the stronger our determination, the more sustainable our confidence will be. Confidence activates the DNA— the Drive, the Nucleus and the Acceleration—that organizes individual effort into a working system of people. It's the dynamics of ODNA with new vitality.[6]

Suzanne Nelson was an unusually resourceful professor of English at The University of Tampa. She enjoyed a good following both as a teacher and as an administrator. This was most notable when she and another professor, Sue McCord who taught social sciences, decided that the University could do a lot of good if it created what they called a "Re-entry Program for Women" who had dropped out of education for family and job reasons, and who needed a more accommodating, confidence-building way to get back to their pursuit of a college degree.[7]

Suzanne also had an active, creative imagination. I was a pipe-smoker at the time, and so was she. We both enjoyed the stylishly easy-to-hold S-shaped variety which, she claimed helped her to ponder the problems at hand. Our administrative team supported them as well as we could, and that program established itself quickly. Confidence is always important to getting ahead, and this was often especially true for upwardly mobile women who needed a better chance.

Then there was Perry Harvey.[8] His was a story of confidence building. He was head of Tampa's longshoreman's union, a close friend of the University's devoted Board Chairman, Bob Thomas, and a savvy gentleman. He and I became friends. He was the University's first black trustee at a time that was not far removed from the last days of segregation on campus.

We decided, with the encouragement of our wives, that we would team up to have some evening socials where leaders from both the black and white communities could get to know each other better. Our thesis was the simple one that better relationships lead to stronger communities. Tampa was then in a state of substantial growth; we wanted to do a good job with building a stronger diverse community and the success of the University depended upon it.

Not long afterward, we began to see more interest in Tampa by members of the black community. They had found new reason to join in building a more diverse community. We sought the assistance of Hillsborough Community College's Vice President of Student Affairs, Barbara Holmes, who became the first black woman to join the UT board. When we re-started varsity basketball at the University, one of its earliest stars was a young black man, Moses Sawney,[9] a friend of our son's who had played ball for a rival high school in Tampa. Moses has since gone on to a successful business career based in Tampa.

Bobbie and I sent our kids to public schools where they not only had black friends, but also black teachers. Blacks began to become an integral part of the Tampa business community and its public life. Confidence continued to grow and Tampa has become an increasingly prosperous city.

The Preamble has the hidden power to give Americans unflagging confidence in their future. For that to happen, we have to abide by it and lead accordingly. Failure to do so risks losing the freedom it confers. We have to believe in it so well that it becomes the civic religion which unleashes the civic virtue of the nation. This deep belief and the actions it impels would apply to the Constitution's designated leaders—the Congress, the President and the Supreme Court—but above all, it would apply to "We the People."

"We the People of the United States" are the source of all power and authority in the country. The people supply the consent of the governed. We go about our daily business not only for ourselves, but also "in Order to form a more perfect Union." This is our responsibility as citizens. This is the purpose and mission of the nation, the soul of the people.

This system of how people think and work, I believe, is in fact a kind of learning organization, as Senge saw it.[10] It recognizes systems thinking in which one sees patterns of behavior through an existential mind map or mental model, whether that mind map is formed deliberately or simply incidentally over time.

The architecture of this freedom mission of the Preamble—"We the people of the United States, in Order to form a more perfect Union"—depends upon the fulfillment of a four-part strategy:

    1) To "establish Justice" creates a foundation of fairness by which all follow the same rules and receive equal treatment;
    2) To "insure domestic Tranquility" allows people to go about their everyday lives in a normal way;
    3) To "provide for the common defence" distances them from both domestic and foreign attack and provides them with protection from the violence of those who would create harm;
    4) To "promote the general Welfare" is to enable the basic necessities and give the opportunity to create some form of abundance for everyone, so no one is left behind.

Taken together, these are the elements of the American strategy. They are the solidarity. Realizing this strategy makes it possible to "secure the Blessings of Liberty." This is the vision and the dream toward which that strategy is directed. It is also the bottom line as the results of this vision and dream extend "to ourselves and our Posterity" over the generations to come.

By crafting this strategy of freedom, the founders affirmed that they "do ordain and establish this Constitution for the United States of America." And in affirming so, they summed up our national purpose.

In stating our national purpose as the first fact of law, the founders were also setting forth what essentially is a national strategy that paves the way of freedom as the solemn and sacred duty of American citizens. This is the core of our security. It carries the persuasive message to prospective partners beyond our borders that they can count on us as we can count on them. Trust.

All of the above must be put in context with the understanding that systems have an indigenous tendency to fail, no matter what they are supposed to be doing or who is supposed to be leading them. That tendency requires the right kind of leadership to make the necessary adjustments for continuous improvement as it goes forward. Therefore, the leaders have to have the talent and ability to empower the rest of the people to follow closely, willingly, and enthusiastically.

Followers and leaders feed off each other. In the ebb and flow of their energy, the critical mass forms and reforms. The preponderance of opinion adjusts and changes. If organized groups are centered in a dynamic mission and share a compelling vision which guide their actions and gather their resources, they will flourish. They will flourish because they are moving forward according to their motives with, not against, the deepest currents of change always going on in the world.

If organized groups do not do follow this process—whether by choice or neglect—they inevitably collapse. They collapse not because they aren't true to their beliefs, but because they don't revise their practices to insure that their message could reach the necessary recipients. This is always tragic to those involved. It need not happen. The requirement is to keep one's feet on the ground, one's eyes on the horizon, and one's mind wide open so one does not miss what's happening as times change. Unfortunately, keeping up with change, and the need thereof, is often a process that is not followed.

The virtue of systems thinking is that it is a holistic approach to an ever-present leadership challenge where there is resistance, and even obstruction, in the path of accomplishment. This often is true all the way from the creation of the vision of a desired future to the actual velocity of getting there. Systems thinking requires big picture focus. It also involves simplification of the complexities and unified support to realize its mission and sustain its impact. When we are able to make the adjustments that are required, we are golden, we get to rule, and we benefit each other in doing so.

Earl Babbie's book, *The Practice of Social Research*[11] was already a best-seller in the academic world when we knew him as our neighbor across the street in Anaheim Hills, California. He and I were colleagues at Chapman University, and he would co-teach a leadership class with me each year. "The only real solutions lie in the ways we organize and run our social affairs," he wrote. Of course, our social affairs include our public affairs and, therefore, our civic life as well.

Earl counseled about how to approach our problems as follows: "The causes lie in the forms, values, and customs that make up organized life and that is where the solutions are hidden." He found that these problems will persist "until we can command our social affairs rather than be enslaved by them." Earl was an ex-Marine as well as a leading academic.

This thought is, for me, a tipping point. Creating freedom requires public law to see that necessary practices become everyday parts of private lives and that such public law be enforced with the full support of the public.

When we consider the Preamble as the beginning of public law, we can link up current issues with its embedded strategies by anchoring them to each specific issue and then networking each issue to all other considerations. For example, a set of current issues might be approached this way:

First, we would begin with the issue of access to quality education every step of the way from childhood, into adulthood, and on to old age. This would enable the most thoughtful society the nation could produce that would, then, address all the other issues from well informed perspectives with the necessary skills.

Second, we would turn to equal voting representation in public elections for all political offices at all levels of government so that the full perspective of all the people is reflected in and by the representatives who then operate in the full interests of all those they serve.

Third, would be to create "equal justice under law" in order to protect the public at large against undue influence obtained in exchange for money or other favors by self-seeking private interests contrary to the public interest.

Fourth, would be to assure safety against domestic terrorism whether it may come from private persons or public officers.

Fifth, would be to protect against foreign terrorism directly affecting American lives wherever they may be.

Sixth, would be to make healthcare accessible for all to enable their most productive participation in the civic life of the nation.

Seventh, would be to grow opportunity for all to search and find jobs and careers that best suit their capacities to serve the greater good.

Eighth, would be to create an optimal infrastructure to enable communication, transportation, and livable communities everywhere for everyone.

This is a proximate list of priorities for law and order in a modern democratic republic. It is not the delirious list of overly serious dreamers or semi-psychos in social bubbles. It is the to-do list for doers. Which are we?

This list is, I believe, an example of what the Preamble's writers would expect if they were around today for a check-up. If the Preamble is to be taken as the mission of freedom by which we are supposed to live, then we must interpret these public standards as well as we know how, in every sector, at every level of public life. The Preamble is a call for straight forward politics. By that I mean politics as a public service, free of playing to the crowd, and for the ultimate good of that crowd. The law is the order for every public servant and every private citizen, to both serve and protect "We the People." The law does start with the Preamble. Right?

VI. BIG PICTURE

Do we have a grand strategy for America? Yes we do. The issue is about implementing it. That is the challenge for political debate.

There is a grand strategy for America's future in freedom.[1] We just don't talk about it. It has the scope and scale that empowers people to address virtually any issue America might face. Our leading statement of law sets forth a national mission with clear strategic parameters.[2] The Preamble of the U.S. Constitution is the core of America's grand strategy.

A startling, beautiful picture of a multi-colored earth in all its unified diversity can be seen from a spacecraft circling the earth. Our solar system is a single planetary system within the greater universe surrounding it. And it is subject to the natural laws which govern that system. While these natural laws don't change, the dynamics of motion that obey them do change.[3] The lesson here is for us to look at the totality of all relevant dynamics whenever we face a problem to be solved. We must do this to avoid being blindsided—as we were on 9-11—by factors unseen yet stoppable if only they are known in time.[4]

The problem, though, is that no single strategy or system of effort alone can get the job done without adjustments made en route to working out the solution and without effective tactics to implement them. Whether it is a system of sure steps, pure information or true ideology, no system by itself can demonstrate its own logical consistency. It is impossible. We know that.

We know it because this is what is demonstrated in Kurt Godel's *Incompleteness Theorem.*[5] He found that no consistent system of truths, no matter how effectively made, is capable of proving all the truth about itself. This also applies to any relationship it has with a different system, including a system or strategy with which it is in conflict.

All information is seen in one's own world, of course, where individuality always makes standardization incomplete, and is limited to the boundaries of its own logic. There is no known set of conditions where a specific body of knowledge will be interpreted in exactly the same way by different people. So, we are left with the uncertainty[6] guaranteed by our incompleteness, and with the need to respect our inherent diversity and interdependence and the need to reconcile differences as best we can.

The Preamble is a statement of mission with a strategy for achieving that mission and a vision of what it will entail when we get there. But, of course, it is not a plan. It is the context within which the picture is painted. Although it is not the picture itself, the Preamble anticipates how the picture may appear as it is being painted. The founders created the original, and ever since, the citizens have been designing a series of reproductions with attention to finer detail in law.

Isaac Asimov[7] was a prolific writer. He could be outrageously funny with statements like:"People who think they know everything are a great annoyance to those of us who do." He had me in stitches late one afternoon as I drove him from the airport to a dinner party where he was about to entertain some of Drew University's generous donors. His point was, of course, that we fallible human beings need to be careful about appearing to know it all when obviously we don't. Even after some 506 books, he admitted he didn't, but he left us all feeling better because we were there with such a sage whose exuberance was contagious.

That is where the golden rule comes in, as the Pope reminded Congress. *Do unto others as you would have them do unto you,* we are told. That way of "doing" has permeated the basic philosophies of all major religions and with good reason. Otherwise there would be constant conflict since no one would trust anyone else. That would obviously be absurd.

I believe we must step forward from the golden rule to an *Nth commandment*. This can be described simply as *"do unto others as you would have them do unto others."* Living that way, you would recognize the needs of others just as you recognize your own needs. Nothing of lasting importance is done alone. Increasing complexity requires more elaborate collaborations. Partnering relationships are increasingly becoming assets of strategic importance beyond what they always have been.

Meanwhile, as we consider our mutuality, we celebrate what we are able to agree upon as workable resolutions of nagging problems. Such resolutions help create a common vocabulary with which to carry on further conversations. Each success, then, leads to further understandings for the settlement of problems that can help in further dialogue. This process then may proceed to the avoidance of war and is more likely to succeed in the presence of peace.

The exchanges that result from this process can produce and reinforce a creative drive that becomes strong enough to generate impulses among different parts of the networked whole which we call the human race. Such a whole, of course, will be responsive to recognized signals. These signals of energy accelerate into sustained currents of strength. They remain so as long as their dots are aligned in demonstrable pictures seen and understood by everyone.

That is why parents teach their children to connect the dots. Then the lines between them become more than just connections. They become the electrified wires of creative energy that lead to what really matters which can be represented by pictures in their minds or on TV or a computer screen. These pictures then become the brighter lights on the dashboards we watch as we navigate our corners of the world.

David Shipler[8] was one of my earliest students. He made it in the world despite struggling with my instruction as a rookie teacher of American history at Chatham High School, New Jersey. David became a distinguished observer, writer and Pulitzer Prize winning author for: *Arab and Jew: Wounded Spirits in a Promised Land*. He acknowledged that, growing up, he had become increasingly interested in connecting the dots to understand the world. He did that very well in class, his teacher notwithstanding.

That is what Americans, indeed all people, more or less learn to do. Connect the dots. See the big picture. We need to do that in spite of whatever limitations we face. In photography, any line is made up of a string of dots. Putting the dots together gives us the path to the goal at the end. We all need help with that. In fact, David's mother, who was a veteran member of the school faculty, was helpful to me in overcoming my own teaching ticks.

Where I live, there are silos aplenty in a lovely countryside of many farms. They are part of a scenic array full of free green pastures, meadows, forests, and hills with an inter-spliced system of roots in mother earth. As Abraham Lincoln said about freedom: it is "the last best hope of earth."[9] The healthier the root system, the greener the countryside. This was the big picture as far as he was concerned. Up here and everywhere, freedom is as green as the sun shines long and the rain comes often enough.

It is from this earth that the sustenance of freedom comes and is nourished. This freedom is what we, as Americans, represent. That's what we believe in. That's what we, each of us with our neighbors, friends and family, must pursue because the last, best hope of the survival and prosperity of this earth is a task that belongs to and benefits all of us.

This leads us to a simple truth: though we may *see* things differently, we *do* things together. That's what a united set of states was created for, and what it does because it must, so it can escape the weakness and decline of a divided set of states. In today's world of instant communication, the good news is that this goal is more readily attainable than it has ever been before. The bad news is that it can also be more readily unraveled and destroyed because of the same circumstances.

So, there must be a climate of support for going forward. That is why negotiated solutions of problems are so important to heal the still undressed wounds of conflict. People at peace do enable the promise of prosperity. People at war do disable that promise. Which do we prefer?

67

What big picture do we have in mind? It makes a difference. Our energy comes from a sense of purpose that finds its way into action. That sense of purpose, however clear or unclear it may seem, is determinative.If we start from a negative attitude, we go negative. If we start from a positive vein, we go positive.

When we began a new "Expanded Curriculum for Excellence in Leadership," or EXCEL as we called it at The University of Tampa, we were assisted by the National Executive Service Corps, and I got to know its founding chairman, Frank Pace, Jr. who was the retired CEO of General Dynamics Corporation and formerly President Harry Truman's Secretary of the Army.

He gave me a copy of a book, *Leaders: The Strategies for Taking Charge,*[10] and recommended the story of Karl Wallenda, the great tightrope walker who suddenly fell to his death from the high wire at age 73. His wife recalled that "All Karl thought about for three straight months prior to it was falling. It was the first time he'd ever thought about that, and it seemed to me that he put all his energies into not falling rather than walking the tightrope." The book's authors, Warren Bennis and Burt Nanus, concluded that when he "poured all his energies into not falling rather than walking the tightrope, he was destined to fall."

The energy of a purpose is powerful. It is the impetus of action and momentum. It's where creativity begins. It's where we are coming from, which frames where we will be heading. As our national statement of purpose, then, the Preamble has a special significance for leading the way toward the future of America.

In *Getting to Yes* by Roger Fisher and William Ury, early leaders of the Harvard Negotiation Project, we learn about how to agree on decision specifics—to carry out our purpose—through negotiation and resolution, when conflict as well as conscience are a big part of the equation, as they so often are.[11] Their approach, which has broad application to most any circumstance, is straightforward: a) clarify the common problem, b) identify the real interests, c) pursue mutual gains, and d) use objective criteria. These are the four essentials. They are the road to success.

When the parties to a dispute agree to come to the table, when they sit down and talk about a problem, they are exploring whether a negotiated agreement can be crafted to solve the problem. They consider why the dispute has become contentious. They understand that there are two sides with opposing views that have created a conflict of interests. They then go on to explore what, exactly, are these interests?

Presumably, there are mutual gains to be had through some sort of dispute resolution. The process explores how such gains can be identified and provided for. And, not to be forgotten, objective criteria need to be agreed upon for purposes of compliance. All this is a tall order to fulfill. Yet, for a return to health, the pills must be taken.

In their work with businesses, government agencies, and civic organizations, the Harvard Project found that the key to success is for each side to know what their bottom line is. The bottom line is that which should also be at the top of their minds.

Wherever the point is—above, below or beyond which we will not go—do we know what and where that is? As Americans, I think we would say it has to do with our freedom. But what does freedom mean to us? Once we define it in a given situation and fix on that, we are in a far stronger position to plan and negotiate whatever the future will be.

Having identified that bottom line, we can take a position from which we won't budge because we have a firm vision in mind that we are not willing to give up. This could not be more powerful. When we have arrived at this place we are strong. When we don't identify this position, we are weak. At best, this vision becomes one that is deeply set in the minds of its holders.

VII. BLIND VISION

"I pledge allegiance to the Flag of the United States of America, and to the Republic for which it stands, one Nation under God, indivisible, with liberty and justice for all."

America's vision is liberty and justice for all. This comes straight from the pledge of allegiance. I dare say that this would be a communion that the Pope could give for more than one nation—for the world.

So goes the pledge we all take, with hand over heart, on occasions of public business and other significant times. How does this vision come into the picture? It's not a dream of what we hope for. It's not a vivid picture of what we are striving for. It is an idea which has meaning. It is what we say about what we believe.

Our ideas start with our imagination. They are not what we see through our eyes when we look out at the world. It's what we see in our minds as we think. This matters because we do actually see ideas with our minds, individually and collectively. We picture our thoughts in our imaginations. And our imaginations dictate our behavior.

This is what the greatest minds have done through the ages. They have imagined what they don't actually see. And they have worked toward what their imaginations want them to see as reality. This is what George Land and Beth Jarman call "future pull."[1] The *pull* of a desired future, they observed, is stronger than the *push* of a less desired past. If this future pull is strong enough, it can be decisive in producing change.

Fredrick Jervis[2] was someone who understood this message. He had a blind vision of the future which was clear enough in his classes. The images he saw were in his mind though they were no longer in his eyes because he had lost his sight in World War II combat. He was a professor of clinical psychology at the University of New

Hampshire when I was a graduate student, and Bobbie and I were newlyweds.

Jervis was also a leadership trainer with an agile imagination who taught that we "back plan" from a dynamic vision that leads us, then we "forward manage" to achieve it. If we try to plan forward from where we are, we are going to focus on the present rather than the future. We will tend to manage for escaping loss rather achieving gain. That virtually guarantees the greater likelihood of falling behind. That is because our focus is the fulcrum. What we concentrate on is what attracts our energy. And the law of gravity kicks in accordingly. The more dynamic that vision is, the more powerfully it is expressed, and the more persuasively it is related to a problem at hand, the more effectively will any organization unify around it and perform efficiently.

Most people start from where they are and then think about where they want to be. But, the improvement of results requires an expansion of efforts, not more of the same. When we feel a strong desire for change and improvement, we rethink the nature of our efforts. The desire energizes the effort and eases the change.

Through the process of back planning and forward managing, Jervis taught that we can plot challenging milestones and surpass them rather than slipping toward tentative targets in tiny steps. He was a good teacher to me as a grad student and years later as a college president. His "planaging model," as he called it, provided a disciplined context for leading management rather than managing leadership. It's an insufficiently recognized difference that can make all the difference in opening up the possibilities of any struggling system. The Jervis planaging model simplified a complex process. Oliver Wendell Holmes, Sr. insightfully observed that: "For the simplicity on this side of complexity, I wouldn't give you a fig. But for the simplicity on the other side of complexity, for that I would give you anything I have."[3] Holmes the elder was a physician, a poet, and author who recognized the value of understanding the core of anything that was complicated. That's what we must do. Sort out the core before we go full bore.

In proposing the Constitution and its Preamble, the founders went through many drafts and had a lot of discussion until they finally reached agreement. They came to it with an extensive knowledge of the Enlightenment that was sweeping across the Europe of that time. They were all Englishmen who had a strong sense of being "heirs to the Enlightenment" as the historian Gordon S. Wood[4] put it. And this attitude was, perhaps, best expressed by the famous words of the Declaration of Independence.

"We hold these truths to be self evident, that all men are created equal, that they are endowed by their Creator with certain unalienable rights, and that among these are Life, Liberty and the pursuit of Happiness."

Unmentioned, but fundamental to these rights, would be the role of learning, both formal and informal, that is acquired at home, in school, or anywhere else. Only a well-informed citizenry would be able to help take responsibility for the quality of life expected in the open society of a republic-at-large. Indeed, only well-informed citizens would be able to perform well and selflessly as servants of the public. Fundamentally, people want to be empowered. Knowledge is power and learning is empowerment. They help engage the natural impulses to live out what people envision and want to experience.

The surgeon turned author, Bernie Siegel, came to the visionary task in a different way. He worked with cancer patients who were at the risk of dying. Some were exceptional in the way they approached their disease which gave him a vision of using love as the best medicine. This approach helped the patients recover through the life-giving miracle of belief in a more purposeful future. It was a simple lesson with power far beyond the threats of disease. It showed how a strong vision of hope can change body chemistry and become a lifestream of energy for anyone in a seriously challenging situation who had not given up.

When, at the suggestion of a mutual friend, I sent him the manuscript of my book, *Leading by Heart,* he replied that it reminded him of what he teaches. I was thrilled. His best-selling book, *Love,*

Medicine and Miracles,[5] had sold millions of copies. What I learned from Bernie, as he asks everyone to call him, was about the physical ramifications of one's spiritual mindset. His work has shown that, in yet mysterious ways, mind changes matter.

Clearly, a mission of freedom today requires well informed citizens who consent to how they are being led. Given this situation, "We the People" will persist through whatever challenges are presented and meet them with sustainable actions and experiences. And that is what America's DNA, in the words of the Preamble, is supposed to do, serving as the basic chemistry of America's body politic. This genetic instinct has led us with the principles of classical republicanism to the practices of democratic capitalism —a process and practice that we're still working on and still struggling with. And, we must keep up the struggle.

A good example was Rebecca Chopp's[6] vision of one small college's future. An institutional plan was created in part on a careful analysis of the college's culture, reflected by its students, faculty and alumni. She commissioned a study of the institution's "DNA," considered a variety of assessments, then went ahead with colleagues to program and build a new library, science hall, and residence complex to address, among other factors, the DNA values found in the study.

The leadership role she was able to take emanated from the plan that came from the people of the community and was not simply an idyllic view for its future. That college is Colgate University, my alma mater, and she was its President. I had earlier sent her a draft of the manuscript of *Leading by Heart* which advanced what I called an organizational DNA or ODNA. She was encouraging and would discuss it with her senior team. She has since gone on to Swarthmore College as President and the University of Denver as chancellor.

Hank Steinbrenner,[7] on the other hand, had not yet gotten clear what his vision was when I knew him as a college student. His dad, George, was then owner of the New York Yankees,[8] and a retired member of the UT Board of Trustees. George always seemed to have a special interest in his own kids. He called me one night and asked if he could bring Hank by the office to say hello before he completed his paperwork for transferring into the University.

The next morning, when we met, we got to talking about the history class I was about to teach on "Mankind at the Turning Point," based, in part, on the much talked about *Second Report to The Club of Rome.*[9] His dad told Hank to sign up for the class which he did, sitting in the front row center every class session.

When I called on him, Hank never gave me the impression he had kept up with the readings, but he always was able to talk about the issues smartly. Academics were not his long suit. But he is the oldest child of an accomplished family. He has gone on to be part-owner and co-chairman of the Yankees, to sponsor "Hank's Yanks" for kids from diverse backgrounds in a summer league of the New York metro area, to play his late father in the movie "Hank and Me" aimed at young boys, and to have four kids of his own. He had acquired a vision, baseball and kids, which is not a bad combination.

In order for a vision to work, it needs to be clear. You have to be able to see it in your mind's eye. It needs to have magnetic resonance in your heart and soul. It is a change-maker. It converts you from being a follower to being an owner. It fills you with a sense of urgency so that you feel a need to take action. Then, you step forward. Your energy level rises. The oxygen flows. You are stronger willed. You become actively engaged.

The difference between one who is so engaged and one who is not is palpable. You can feel the thrust that is created by having this impelling vision. It is not only self-propelling, it radiates to others and penetrates their energy fields. They become energized by the same vision and join in. This is leadership happening. When it comes to our public leaders, we unfortunately do not see enough of this type of leadership—as distinct from showmanship. That failure of leadership weakens our freedom because it does not improve our choices and, therefore, reduces our prospects of moving forward as a compelling and sustainable vision is aimed at doing.

Pope Francis saw the strength of the type of vision displayed by the Reverend Dr. Martin Luther King, Jr. in his dream of full civil and political rights for African-Americans. "That dream," the Pope said in his address to Congress, "continues to inspire us all."[10] He then continued: "millions of people came to this land to pursue their dream of building a future in freedom." And these people have played enormous roles in the growth and development of the country.

So long as America's vision and practice of freedom attracts foreigners to our land, and so long as we wish to earn the good will of people from other nations, we can expect to be judged by the way we meet the continuing challenge of how we welcome strangers to our midst, and what this says to the world about the power of our legitimacy as a land of freedom.

One of my mother's favorite songs was "America the Beautiful" written by Katharine Lee Bates.[11] Her visionary words were especially meaningful. Think of the Preamble as you read them.

O beautiful for spacious skies,
For amber waves of grain,
For purple mountains majesties
Above the fruited plain!

We the People of the United States

America! America!
God shed His grace on thee,
And crown thy good with brotherhood
From sea to shining sea!

in Order to form a more perfect Union

O beautiful for pilgrim feet
Whose stern impassioned stress
A thoroughfare for freedom beat
Across the wilderness.

75

establish Justice

America! America!
God mend thine ev'ry flaw,
Confirm thy soul in self control,
Thy liberty in law.

insure domestic Tranquility

O beautiful for glorious tale
Of liberating strife,
When valiantly for man's avail
Men lavish precious life.

provide for the common defence

America! America!
May God thy gold refine
Till all success be nobleness,
And ev'ry gain divine.

promote the general Welfare

O beautiful for patriot dream
That sees beyond the years
Thine alabaster cities gleam
Undimmed by human tears.

and secure the Blessings of Liberty

America! America!
God shed His grace on thee,
And crown thy good with brotherhood
From sea to shining sea.

To ourselves and our Posterity.

When we take a close look at the phrases and see the message of the Preamble ringing through the symphonious phrases of the song: "O beautiful for spacious skies" …"Crown thy good with brotherhood"…"O beautiful for pilgrim feet—a thoroughfare for freedom beat" "Confirm thy soul in self control, Thy liberty in law;" "Till all success be nobleness;" "O beautiful for patriot dream…undimmed by human tears." No wonder our love for this country and for each other is enhanced.

VIII. FREEDOM GATES

What does freedom's history teach? First, negative freedom—from autocracy. Then, positive freedom—for democracy.

From the point of view of the law, America's freedom traces back to the Magna Carta, 800 years old in 2015.[1] This is the oldest charter of freedom in the recorded history of the world. It was prepared by the Archbishop of Canterbury for King John of England to grant protection for rebellious feudal barons from illegal imprisonment, denial of justice, and excess taxation.

The protection and rights granted by the Magna Carta were to be enforced by a council of peers, not the monarch himself, who was a tyrant afraid of his own supplicants. This document was a first for peace with freedom in the world, even though it was granted by a king only to his mutinous barons, and then wrangled over for years afterward.

The Magna Carta is nevertheless considered the foundation for resisting arbitrary authority by despots such as the king. Because it seemed to touch the core instincts of humankind and helped shape Enlightenment thinking in Europe,[2] the Magna Carta later influenced the formulation of the U.S. Constitution, helping America to escape the aristocratic rule of monarchy and replace it with the representative democracy of a republic. This lit a fire for freedom across the world.

The earliest formulation of freedom in America may have been the unsung 1640 "Freedom of Conscience Agreement,"[3] the drafting of which was led by the Reverend Roger Williams and agreed to by the lay people of the Providence Plantation, now the state of Rhode Island. By that agreement, everyone in the territory was grante vbn.d freedom of religion, of thought and of expression. Their beliefs, ideas, and actions were protected so long as they did no harm to another. This was a cornerstone of individual freedom, separation of church and state, and majoritarian democracy all at once.

America's Declaration of Independence from England in 1776 proclaimed a message of expectation and uplift as written by Thomas Jefferson, and was a clear and present influence on his friend from Virginia, James Madison, who both oversaw and personally undertook the draftsmanship of the Constitution with help especially from Gouverneur Morris of New York.

After the failure of the Articles of Confederation to hold the divided states together in a shell government called the "United States", the new Constitution was drafted in 1787 and submitted to the thirteen states for ratification which was finally completed in 1789. The first sentence of that document was the "Preamble," which introduced the Law of the Land by proclaiming that:

"We the People of the United States, in Order to form a more perfect Union, establish Justice, insure domestic Tranquility, provide for the common defence, promote the general Welfare, and secure the Blessings of Liberty, to ourselves and our Posterity, do ordain and establish this Constitution for the United States of America."

That is a good summation of the "American Idea," as historian Gordon Wood has explained it.[4] This is what we were to be about. Upon this foundation, it was hoped, we have a way forward on which to stake our reputation. All the law that its prophets would need to know flows from this idea and its precepts. Legal interpretations would need to take its spirit and meaning into account in all cases. Congressional law would need to follow along accordingly. And presidential decision-making would need to reflect its integrity. The government would resolve whatever inferences might arise.

The first ten amendments were added to the Constitution in 1791 by the Bill of Rights.[5] These amendments spelled out how the promises of the Preamble and the Articles would begin to translate into the rights of the people. The best known of the ten was the First Amendment:

"Congress shall make no law respecting an establishment of religion, or prohibiting the free exercise thereof; or abridging the freedom of speech, or of the press; or the right of the people peaceably to assemble and to petition the Government for a redress of grievances."

Also well known is the Second Amendment:

"A well regulated Militia, being necessary to the security of a free State, the right of the people to keep and bear Arms, shall not be infringed."

The Civil War's aftermath was critical for the cause of freedom in America. The Emancipation Proclamation by President Abraham Lincoln in 1863[6] led to the abolition of slavery by the Thirteenth Amendment in 1865.[7] Freedom was then bolstered by the equal protection clause of the Fourteenth Amendment in1868.[8] The institution of slavery was America's "great sin," as it has become known, from the early years of its settlement by Europeans. Freedom *from* slavery was a step of negative freedom on the road *to* democracy, which was a step of positive freedom. Freedom of action would require both steps.

The other landmark amendment for freedom was the Nineteenth which came in 1920 when women's suffrage finally came of age in the aftermath of World War I.[9] That Amendment presumably gave half of America's census population the right to vote. Since then, women have gradually, and recently far more rapidly, moved toward full equality under the law.

The relationship of women with the rise of what the world has come to recognize as a "knowledge society" has not been fully recognized.[10]There is increasing evidence to show that females tend to develop their intellectual gifts earlier than males[11]for very basic reasons since pre-historic times, through recorded history.

Women have also tended to assume peacemaking roles more consistently than do men who have been the protectors and the providers. In looking at the roles of leadership today, it is clear that both knowledge and reconciliation are crucial for truth to abide, even as verification remains what it always has been, a necessity for trust to last.

Francis Fukuyama[12] has written most clearly about the practicality of "Trust" in his book on that subject. Trust is a key factor in keeping people together and functioning productively. Plain talk about trust and productivity leaves the bluster about toughness and triumph behind.

This acknowledgement represents a monumental recognition of the actual role women have always played in the world despite the resistance of those who have insisted that manpower should be taken as literal truth. They forget that literacy is a term of description, not of truth. And isn't that what the law requires of us: "The truth, the whole truth, and nothing but the truth"?

Franklin D. Roosevelt was the President who spoke in his First Inaugural about the underlying role that fear plays in the equation of freedom—"the only thing we have to fear is fear itself—nameless, unreasoning, unjustified terror which paralyzes needed efforts to convert retreat into advance." Roosevelt's later "Four Freedoms" speech came during the lead-up to World War II and was persuasive in steeling the resolve of Americans about the choices ahead. He emphasized that freedom of speech and expression, freedom of every person to worship God in his own way, freedom from want, and freedom from fear are essentials for people everywhere in the world, not just America.[13]

This kind of world, FDR said, would be the anti-thesis of the new order of tyranny that the Nazis, Fascists, and Communists of that time were threatening. He envisioned a moral order creating a good society able to face the schemes of world domination without fear. The absence of fear makes room for the presence of compassion that always has been fundamental to the human condition and the duality of human nature.

It's time, actually way past time, to learn history in order to escape another tyranny of aristocracy — this time by a deep-pocketed small minority of extremely wealthy individuals supporting a political class sitting atop a rigged constitutional system which has our nation in its grip as it sours the lives and stokes the fears of everyday Americans.[14] It is time to revisit the Preamble, the source of America's organizing purpose of freedom. That freedom is embedded in the American DNA. It includes both the negative freedom from slavery as well as the positive freedom to exercise inalienable rights. Here is where America's unique genetic program and its greatest strengths lie.

Howard Schultz, the Starbucks CEO, recently pointed out that: "The common purpose that created this great nation, which has united us in difficult moments, has gone missing."[15] Yes, it is past time that we take a closer look at America's statement of national purpose. And, yes, again, the Preamble is the document that sends America on its mission and sets forth a strategy to achieve it.

Our vision of freedom is the big reason why we have successfully grown into a continental republic of more than three hundred million people that began as a coastal colony of three million people, who lived over three thousand miles across the Atlantic from the seat of an Empire that ruled it almost three centuries ago.

By many measures, we are the strongest nation in the world today.[16] But we are also a nation that faces some clear and present dangers that we have failed to find lasting solutions for, however hard we try to put them behind us. During my days at the Center for Strategic & International Studies (CSIS), I served with Jim Woolsey, the future CIA director under President Bill Clinton who was then legal counsel at CSIS.

He never lost an opportunity to remind us about the "clear and present danger" of perceived threats to America's national security.[17] The real problem we never talked about, though, was that we were not prompted by our common ground in the Preamble. Neither was anyone else. We talked incessantly about security, and we worked hard at dialogue regarding security. They were our great strength.

But there was no real focus on how to "secure the Blessings of Liberty" as a grand strategy for America. It was never more than a side issue, rather than the national purpose for which we worked. Nobody seemed to be seriously considering that. We were not taking advantage of it as the basis for solving America's most strategic problems then, and we are not doing so now.

Our hyper-partisan politics encourage those who perceive our lack of unity as a weakness they can exploit. That does threaten our freedom. We can do better. The framework of law and order we need is set forth in the first sentence of the Constitution.

As a nation whose leadership starts in Washington, we need to work smarter than we have been. And we need to be better in order to last longer. If pride is what drives us, then let's employ it for getting to solutions. We believe in freedom. We do freedom. Freedom is the mission. Safety is the result. It is not the other way around. Fire keeps us warm. Fear keeps us cold.

Eleanor Roosevelt led the drafting of a Universal Declaration of Human Rights in 1948,[18] which was agreed upon by the United Nations General Assembly with only the Soviet bloc opposed. It was a statement of moral principles with no provision for its enforcement, and it has been given little recognition ever since. Just not newsworthy enough? We need to change that.

This Declaration proclaims a "common standard of achievement for all peoples and all nations." It sets forth a canon of rights and freedoms that "every individual and every organ of society, keeping this declaration constantly in mind, shall strive by teaching and education to promote respect for." Any pope or president would applaud such a canon.

This Declaration begins with the statement that "All human beings are born free and equal in dignity and rights. They are endowed with reason and conscience and should act toward one another in a spirit of brotherhood." It goes on to elaborate what the members meant in a set of thirty specific articles of rights and freedoms. In adopting these, the members of the United Nations General Assembly were laying a foundation upon which the world could build a more promising future after the atrocities of death and destruction in World War II.

It is interesting to note that the words and meanings in the Universal Declaration arose from a committee of nations chaired by an American woman, that much of its language is a reflection of the Declaration of Independence, the U.S. Constitution and the Bill of Rights, that the work was completed in San Francisco and goes on in New York City at the United Nations. America and its allies had won the war. Having prevailed in war, they wanted to win the peace.

IX. AMERICA'S PURPOSE

Is ours a "Preamble of Freedom?" It is our first fact of law. It is not yet our living fiber of life. It can win hearts and minds in the world.

As we have seen, America's national purpose is stated in the Preamble—the heart of our nation.[1] Such a statement makes clear where one is coming from and then points toward where one is planning to go, creating a good idea of what it will take to get there. This is what the Preamble does as the first fact of law in the United States of America.

The founder's purpose and plan for the law of the land clearly was based on the idea of creating a free country, independent of rule by a foreign power. The introductory words in the Preamble were certainly intended to set forth the main features of the body politic to which the Constitution was giving birth.

These words put forward a simple statement of purpose, where the Founders were coming from, so to speak. Its role as a statement of mission is to make clear the substance they had in their hearts and minds. The people, not the king and his court, were to be the authority. Their task would be to create a more perfect union of all those who would be part of the body.

These words are the reflections of a collective soul—that of the founders— intended to lead a new nation. As they saw it, "We the People of the United States, in Order to form a more perfect Union:"

- would need to "establish Justice" so that there would be fair play and equal treatment according to law;
- would need to "insure domestic Tranquility" so that communal disputes would not disrupt the everyday social intercourse of human relations;
- would need to "provide for the common defence" in order to protect the safety of families and children, friends and neighbors from attack by foreign invaders;

- would need to "promote the general Welfare" to enable people to prosper, be productive, and serve the country.

All of these actions would be essential to "secure the Blessings of Liberty" that would be doubtful, if not impossible, without them. And they would provide that "to ourselves and their Posterity" because easy fixes could be so easily undone and distract people from their pursuits of life, liberty and happiness.

In the time of our founding, people did not use the term sustainability. Make no mistake, however, in setting out the idea of forming this more perfect union as an independent state, the founders wanted to provide it with the capacity to sustain itself. Their use of the word "Posterity" refers to the following generations that would be coming of age. The idea of posterity anticipates that the sweep of the future, not just the surges of tomorrow, is to be kept well in mind when doing the work of the people. Mindfulness is mighty powerful alongside its absence. Loss of hearts and minds leads to loss of life and times.

There were two routes on the way in to Yogi Berra's house in New Jersey, and you could take either one. So, he'd tell friends coming for the first time: "*When you come to a fork in the road, take it.*"[2] He meant what he said, but he didn't necessarily say it so clearly. Literalists take note! He meant that when there are choices, you get to decide and you go from there. These, then, are words of wisdom for Americans deciding which fork in the road our country should take.

In our lives, we often come to a fork related to choosing a course of action that begins in a certain place. Should we simply choose to move on from where we are and where we're coming from? Or would it help in making the decision to know where we want to get to -- where we actually want to be? In the latter case, we would have a picture in mind that would at least partially and more positively describe our desired landing place. The clearer that picture becomes, the greater is its effect on our choice of direction for reaching our goal.

Jack Hennessey[3] had a quiet and compelling message. A "force multiplier,"[4] in military terminology, is born of a clear mission which is incorporated in a broad vision. He was a four-star General who led the U.S. Readiness Command at MacDill Air Force Base in Tampa when we invited him, upon his retirement, to accept a seat on our Board of Trustees at The University of Tampa. Having had a successful career in the nation's service, Jack knew what he was needed for. His job was to see to it that U.S. forces, wherever they were stationed in the world, had the supplies necessary to do their jobs. He knew how to do that.

In subsequent planning discussions with Board members, he explained the essence of how force multipliers, whatever their nature, are the outcomes of careful calculation—which one shall we choose? They are driven by the morale of believing leaders and participants. Choosing a force multiplier is a way of marshaling all available resources behind a clear purpose that supports a compelling vision of the future.

A force multiplier dramatically improves the effectiveness of a group. It is the DNA of an integrated system and has great power. It drives the system forward, helps form a growing nucleus of action, and increases the velocity of its acceleration with lightning effect. The force multiplier is the power that determines the outcome. That's why it is such a favored term of strategists plotting how missions can be accomplished. Clearly stating the mission and its goals well is its first significant requirement. The Preamble is America's force multiplier.

Frederick Jervis,[5] the blind professor and leadership trainer at the University of New Hampshire, defined a mission as making clear its distinguishing features, who it serves, and what it should accomplish. It should be simply stated, readily remembered, with enough drawing power to lead the people who are responsible for interpreting it while using the best of means to fulfill its high purpose. This high purpose is the force multiplier. If it is unclear, it becomes the force divider. The preamble as force multiplier is a long sentence with a short message—freedom.

America's doctrine of freedom, found in the Preamble, is the basis of our charter authority as a nation. It is the frame of reference of our reputation. Since 1776, our leaders have envisaged the United States as a free country in a world to be set free. Our leadership is intimately linked to following it. Leadership, lest we forget, always follows a cause, which is an idea that compels people to act. This is true for all people. Our cause is this freedom. It will save us. It always has. It always will *if* we follow it.

In 1776, freedom was uncommon. In fact, it was virtually nonexistent in governmental terms anywhere in the then known civilized world.[6] Today, unfreedom is still strangely common, though not talked about in so many words, even in the United States. There are a number of components of this lack of freedom:

- Not having supportive parenting or families;
- Not having proper food and clothing;
- Not having adequate shelter;
- Not having the money for necessities;
- Not having the strength to be sociable;
- Not knowing what to do or how;
- Giving up and dropping out.

Each and all of these, especially the last, subtract from freedom. They are the ingredients of unfreedom. They beget anxiety and frustration, even rage and violence. In America, unfreedom should be abnormal. Abnormal can be unhealthy, and unhealthy is unproductive. No one is in favor of America being unproductive. Is there a surer way to plot our own demise? It is imperative that Americans are productive citizens all.

We get more problems when we take less responsibility. Do we cherish the flare ups? Then we should forget our civility. Are we not angered by disturbance? Then we don't need to pay attention. Are we blameful of others? Then we might ask ourselves why.

Thoughtfulness is necessary before it is nice. In a busy world, full of distraction, there is something we can all do well to practice:

discipline! That is not a pleasant thought? It is a life saver. Being disciplined does not contradict also being a free spirit—it simply dictates what one is being disciplined about. Without discipline, we are wild; with it, we are civilized. At its best, it is self-imposed. It is the mark of a free person.

Abraham Lincoln summed it up as in his Second Message to Congress as President: "In giving freedom to the slave we assure freedom to the free, the last best hope of earth."[7] That, for America, and for us, would be the simple truth. We can find what we want, if we can remember what we don't want.

Mangosuthu Buthelezi[8] visited The University of Tampa when he was King of the Zulus in South Africa. Virtually unknown to Americans, he was first a political adversary of Nelson Mandela and then a political collaborator. His diligent efforts to help free all the people of South Africa rested on his deep belief in their being educated to be able to take on the new responsibilities of independence. It was my honor to present him with his first honorary degree in America. My wife Bobbie was sitting with his wife who wept as a white South African student of ours rose to thank him for his words of response as a voice of that beloved country's future. Though Buthelezi traveled with a retinue of aides, all he needed on campus was the truth of his message. He was a blessing to us.

Over time there has been an erosion of America's mission of freedom, a common and often deadly organizational disease in countries, communities, and all kinds of corporations, for profit and not-for-profit. We are not educating people about the Preamble or reminding them of it or holding them to account for it. In every respect, America's independence and its leadership of the world depend upon our adherence to the Preamble's coherence. Unity in a mission is always essential for an organization to move forward, whether within a neighborhood, within a nation or within a nuclear family.

The progress of this unity in a mission is akin to the rolling of a rock which picks up creative energy and critical mass moving down a hill at great speed as it becomes an increasingly unstoppable force. It's like an invisible DNA that grows and grows, one way or another, as it goes and goes, this way and that. This is true unless the DNA is neglected, as America's has been. Contrary powers then fill the vacuum. And that is perhaps the deepest threat that faces us now. Maybe we should worry a little less about our foreign enemies and a little more about national suicide.

Our President is sworn to serve America's purpose, as is the Congress and the Supreme Court. The question is, as always, how that mission is interpreted and supported. When all is said and done, as Lincoln said, "In giving freedom to the slave we assure freedom to the free."

The Preamble is the first fact of America's law and its statement of national purpose. When America was a caterpillar, the Preamble changed it into a butterfly and the world was never the same. Butterflies have been doing transformations in all recorded history. America can, too, as long as it remembers who it is and continues to reproduce itself as a butterfly nation. Yes, as Charles Dickens said and the Broadway play proclaimed, butterflies are free. They give birth to caterpillars who grow up.

X. HISTORIC DAY

Do leaders make a difference? Consider unprecedented political forgiveness and unprecedented political terror on the same day.

Whoever our President is makes a great deal of difference. The content of one's character always does, whether we are talking about a President or anyone else. And that content, of course, differs from moment to moment, person by person. If we pay close attention, we will usually notice a remarkable consistency present in each one. When making a choice, then, it is always wiser to support the one we think will do the most good as distinct from the one we might personally like best.

The President is the leader of the government, and the government is there to do what we are unable to do by ourselves.[1] Without the government, we'd be back to the laws of the jungle. That is why we have the laws of the land to benefit the whole of the body politic. That is also why we do ourselves a huge favor when we pay enough attention to realize what is actually happening behind the scenes.

William Shakespeare famously exalted that: "All the world's a stage."[2] He was right—partially right—that is. There is always a great deal going on off stage, behind the scenes, the part we don't see and, therefore, have to investigate if we want to know the whole story. Maybe the whole story isn't important, but when we are talking about the future of the United States, especially if we are worried and complaining about it, it would be helpful to know and understand what really is going on.

The playhouse and the movie theater, the newspapers and the radio, and now cable television and social media, play forcefully into the popular culture. Information overload is old news. How do we separate the wheat from the chaff; the meat from the fat; the facts from the fiction; the bull from the beef? It's getting harder to do. We get information faster, but it takes more time and thought to distill it because there is so much more of it.

T.S. Eliot put it artfully in *Choruses from the Rock*[3] when he lamented:

> *"Where is the Life we have lost in living?*
> *Where is the wisdom we have lost in knowledge?*
> *Where is the knowledge we have lost in information?*
> *The world turns and the world changes,*
> *But one thing does not change.*
> *In all of my years, one thing does not change…*
> *The perpetual struggle of Good and Evil."*

Few, if any, days in American history have had a greater coincidence of significance with less notice than September 8, 1974.[4] On that day on the world's stage, an American President was pardoned by his successor for a crime against the people, and an American passenger plane was bombed out of the air by international terrorists. One was an act of unprecedented political forgiveness. The other was an act of unprecedented political terror. Both were firsts. Both commanded front page newspaper headlines the next day across the world. The first remained in the news. The second disappeared. There were important considerations for freedom in both cases.

Gerald Ford was a forgiving man. That character trait was a blessing and a curse. As President of the United States, he publicly pardoned a crime against his own nation that had significant effect. And then, on the same day, he publicly neglected another crime against his nation and other nations, a crime whose reverberations continue to this day.

Although I had the honor of hosting President Ford for an address at The University of Tampa after he had left the Presidency, I've lamented my hesitation to ask him about the aftermath of the bombing of that plane on that day he pardoned Nixon. My brother, former USAF Captain Jon L. Cheshire, was the plane's co-pilot. Given the former President's schedule, there was no private time to raise the question. I let it go.

President Richard Nixon's pardon by President Gerald Ford occurred several hours after the crash of TWA flight 841 in the Ionian Sea off the coast of Greece. It was the first terrorist bombing of an American passenger plane in flight. As it happened, I had earlier met President Nixon at a White house function. Later at a CSIS function, I met Alexander Haig who is said to have proposed the pardon to President Ford. The black box with critical flight information was left 10,000 feet under the sea and with it was lost any clues that might have helped prevent future disasters.

A couple of decades later, Patty Cheshire, wife of my nephew Devon, Jon's son, came to the conclusion that it made no sense to leave such a family tragedy unexplained, as it largely had been, if there was any helpful information that could be found. She dug up press clippings, got hold of official reports, and never let it fall far from her mind.

One day she met a woman whose husband, incredibly, had been on the first rescue ship to arrive at the crash site. Her husband, who had since become a senior pilot for U.S. Air, recounted the nightmares he had been having ever since. Over dinner one evening at Devon and Patty's home, he lamented the loss of evidence that went down to the sea bottom in the cockpit of the plane. "It would surely have helped to prevent future horrors like this one," he thought.

Then she met another woman whose husband's mother and younger brother were passengers on the plane. Her husband recounted the story of their peace mission to Israel from which they were returning. The mother was an activist who was seeking a greater understanding of life in a new country not yet at peace with its neighbors. Over another meal in their home, we heard about the loss of an informed voice who "could have made more of a difference to a world in conflict," as her son said.

It was only afterward that Patty discovered Mike Finnegan,[5] the retired FBI agent who had actually tracked down the suspected bomb maker. Mike hasn't given up his devotion to the cause of counterterrorism. When he spoke with our family, he likened the pursuit of terrorists to being "wise as a serpent and gentle as a dove," as the biblical story goes. His interpretation of America's fight for freedom pays full respect both to the supremacy of our values and to the smartness of our fight. We must be resourceful and relentless on behalf of civilization itself.

Yet, a pattern of neglect has been a big part of why we need to return to the Preamble of the Constitution. This first fact of law indicates that our national purpose is to secure our freedom as a civic people. We are to be a civic nation that prospers according to collective works and common wisdom. We would be united Americans who act with civic virtue. Our leaders would understand how the wisdom of the people should engage their leadership. And we would listen for the dreaming of whatever beyond the screaming of whomever.

Few leaders have inspired my wonderment about the future more than the reputedly bombastic inventor of the hydrogen bomb. I spent most of a day with Edward Teller on a trip to Cape Kennedy when he was my guest in Tampa. Teller was gracious, thoughtful, and plain spoken through his thickly accented words about America's role in the world.

His book *The Pursuit of Simplicity*[6] later inspired me to reexamine my thoughts about how we ought to address the future of a civilized society. The whole experience with Teller was humbling, getting to visit with the inventor of the world's most powerful bomb about the world's most volatile peace made an everlasting impression on me. How is it that such differences—war and peace, conflict and conciliation—can reside in one person? Yet they do, I suspect, in great and small ways, in all of us.

In order to regain our balance as a nation it's very important that we understand what freedom means for us now. It's not too much to say, I believe, that the Preamble of the Constitution is also a "Preamble of Freedom" for the World. That imposes a special responsibility on all of us who are fortunate enough to be American citizens. We have a duty to accept that responsibility.

When we think about our world, however we define it, it helps to remember that it is both diverse and unitary at the same time. It also helps if we can think of it as greater than the sum of its parts. Our planet, for example, is composed of interdependent parts which work more or less together as a greater whole that supports life. This is significant because we do well to see the big picture before we agree on proposals to solve problems that arise inside it. Failing this approach, we endanger our chances, both of solving the problem, and enhancing our strength, at the same time. Thus, our involvement in the Israeli-Palestinian conflict, and the fallout from that involvement, is a case-in-point.

Sam Wanamaker[7] and Ronald Reagan[8] were both born in Illinois and both became actors in Hollywood. Sam was a former Communist who became the expatriate American who led the UK-based Shakespeare's Globe Theatre historic reconstruction project that had world outreach ambitions. Former President Reagan was an outspoken anti-Communist who became an activist global leader, and later, Honorary Chair of that Globe Theater project in America when I was its stateside director.

On this project, at least, the two former actors were simpatico. They worked well together. They enjoyed each other's company. They cut a videotape which would highlight the importance of Shakespeare's Globe to the world. If they could collaborate on a project of this nature, I thought, we can follow their example for broader projects. The trick, of course, was that they knew and respected each other, and they had something in common. It's amazing what can be done once those ingredients meet in the same place. For that to happen, an attitude of mutuality is essential. These men had that.

Forgiveness is a terribly under-appreciated attribute and under-used way of operating successfully. This is much to humanity's loss. "Forgive them their sins for they know not what they do," Jesus said as he hung dying on the cross.[9] That is a message that knows no specific faith, only faith itself. Faith in forgiveness stands on its own, whatever ground of faith we stand on.

Abraham Lincoln knew that as President. In the closing lines of his Second Inaugural Address he said these immortal words that are now carved in stone on his memorial in Washington D.C.:

"With malice toward none; with charity for all; with firmness in the right, as God gives us to see the right, let us strive on to finish the work we are in; to bind up the nation's wounds; to care for him who shall have borne the battle, and for his widow, and his orphan-- to do all which may achieve and cherish a just, and a lasting peace, among ourselves, and with all nations."[10]

The gift of forgiveness is to achieve freedom without a fight. The benefit of forgiveness is a release of the soul from the chains of hatred, from the shame of retribution and from the blood of war. The cost of unforgiveness is walking with rotten crutches while boasting disgraceful pride. This is why we sing "Amazing Grace"[11] and weep with tears of sorrow. Only reconciliation can save us from ourselves. If only we could remember that when we get upset with those who think differently. It would be easier to quit feeling sorry for ourselves and self-righteous about others.

XI. TOP TEN

Is the Preamble our soul? It is our national purpose. It is the heart of the nation. It is the core of America's grand strategy.

The spirit of the Constitution is too often dimly reflected in the application of law today. In The Federalist No. 81, Alexander Hamilton said "The power of construing the laws according to the spirit of the Constitution, will enable [the Supreme Court] to mold them into whatever shape it may think proper."[1] What he didn't mention, and perhaps might not have imagined, was how influential public opinion would be with the Court and how it could factor into the ideological equations of justice that have played an important role ever since.[2]

Are "We the People"—led by our law makers, our public administrators, and our judiciary system—following the lead of that law? Well, there is reason to say no, they are not. And I presume to think that Professor Jervis, blind vision and all, would agree. Why would this be my observation? Because we are not living up to the obligations spelled out in our Preamble of freedom.[3]

Service to our country as a normal and acceptable duty does not pack much power with as many as it must if we are to keep it free. "To accept your country without betraying it, you must love it for that which shows what it might become. America—this monument to the genius of ordinary man and woman, this place where hope becomes capacity, this long, halting turn of the 'no' into the 'yes'—needs citizens who love it enough to re-imagine and remake it."[4] These are the prophetic words of professor Cornel West of Union Theological Seminary.

The Preamble is the heart and soul of America, the spirit of the law. Since there is no stopping the human spirit when it is fully present, we need to be sure that it keeps us company all along our journey. If "The American Spirit" is embedded in the Preamble, then we must call it out, nurture it, and work it up to the forefront of the road ahead. So, let's take a closer look, point-by-point.

Point one: "We the People of the United States" refers to private citizens acting freely and democratically in what is intended to be a constitutional republic. Does it make sense that the influence of the big money of a few should outweigh a one-person-one-vote standard in the election of public officials? This goes back to the Supreme Court's ruling for the so-called "equal protection clause" in 1964.

Is the welfare of the people or the preservation of property the first concern of government? Is money itself a form of property? Is the use of money a form of speech? Can it be equated with a person? Can the wealth and power of a publicly chartered organization be used to override the constitutional rights of its people?

The first words which authorize all the law of our land are "We the People." They are known by everyone, though the rest of the sentence that follows them are not. Why is that? Because these words and the principles they stand for haven't been taught. Not by lawyers and judges. Not by politicians and pundits. Not even by teachers and professors. Not really. Why?

These first three words and the next four dozen words of the U.S. Constitution's Preamble constitute the genesis, the exodus, and the revelation of law in America. Do we believe in the Constitution? It starts here. Do we want law and order? It starts here. Do we believe that our republic is a form of democracy? It starts here.

The meaning of these opening words is that "We the People" are the first and last authority upon which our law rests and it is for us that it serves. We are the living human beings whose assent as the governed was inscribed for all time by Thomas Jefferson in the Declaration of Independence. It is American citizens who are responsible for the law under which they live. That is why it is so important that we learn about that law, how it is created and applied, how we can evaluate those outcomes, and how we can most effectively act in response to it.

Reference to "the United States" is not to be taken for granted. The founders chose that term rather than one connoting a confederation of divided states. They chose it because the challenge they faced was to form a national identity. This greater identity, enshrining the collectivity of thirteen former colonies into the unity of one, singular nation, was intended to elevate their power to serve and protect their citizens more effectively than they otherwise could.

Thus, the whole was to be greater than the sum of the parts. The whole could do what the parts could not alone do for their citizens. The rights and responsibilities of the people would then supersede those of the states and their people alone when it comes to questions with direct implications for the nation as a whole.

Voting can well illustrate the issue. Let us agree that the perpetuation of our democracy in the name of freedom does indeed require a truly representative republic. Remember Ben Franklin's response to the question about having a monarchy or a republic? "A republic, if you can keep it," he replied. This being the case, who would disagree?

TIME's 2012 gala for the magazine's "100 most influential people" included the billionaire David Koch and the comedian Stephen Colbert. In his speech before the attendees Colbert said: "I was particularly excited to meet David Koch earlier tonight because I have a Super PAC, and I am—thank you, thank you—happy to announce Mr. Koch has pledged $5 million to my Super PAC. And the great thing is, thanks to federal election law, there's no way for you ever to know whether that's a joke. By the way, if David Koch likes his waiter tonight, he will be your next congressman."[4]

Paul Volcker considered himself first and foremost a public servant. As Chairman of the Federal Reserve Board he was devoted to public service above and beyond other considerations. Known as the "gentle giant" at six feet even inches tall, and a graciously disciplined private person, Volcker happened to be the first to greet Bobbie and me after my appointment at CSIS when we arrived at our first official function. Later, his responsiveness to the briefings that I assisted with, as he assumed the Chairmanship of the Center's Advisory Board, were as memorable to me as they were ordinary to him. He was known as a leader who focused on doing the right thing as a public official, and also in prominent roles as a private citizen, and it was more than refreshing to experience that attitude so directly.

"What's the subject of life —to get rich?"[6] Volcker once asked. "All of those fellows out there getting rich could be dancing around the real subject of life." He was especially concerned about the special interests that were obstructing political policy-making: "The worse thing is the money in Washington," he said. "I am disappointed in the system and how it has become so polarized."[7] His reputation has never been tarnished by scandal. The Telegraph of London reported that he questioned "how much of the Wall Street boom years had actually translated into tangible wealth for wider society—in terms of economic productivity and growth in GDP?" An exceptional American leader.

Point two: The next words of our first sentence, "in Order to form a more perfect Union," refer to leading a federation of united states instead of a confederation of divided states. They sum up the simple purpose of the law. They state what the Constitution was established to do. They lead directly to the principles we must value to pursue that purpose. And they make it clear that we must be unified in order to be strong in the pursuit of our purpose as a new nation. Our union would be necessary to keep us free.

These words acknowledged the divisions among the states and with the union itself at that time, and led to the need for the creation of a more perfect union in the first place. Today, some of those divisions still exist among the states and the protection of fair and impartial access to voting for all citizens in the elections of public officials is still an issue. Is not the guarantee of equal voting rights—access, counting, reporting—pre-eminently important to preserve democracy, and therefore the duty of the courts to serve and the states to protect?

As John Jay, the first Chief Justice of the Supreme Court, wrote in The Federalist No. 2,

> *"It is worthy of remark that not only the first, but every succeeding Congress, as well as the late*

convention, have invariably joined with the people in thinking that the prosperity of America depended upon its union. To preserve and perpetuate it was the great object of the people in forming that convention, and it is also the great object of the plan which the convention has advised them to adopt. "[8]

William Rogers, as U.S. Attorney General, was an exemplar of law and order in civil rights cases, such as those involving public school at Little Rock. "It seems inconceivable," he said, "that a state or community would rather close its public schools than to comply with decisions of the Supreme Court."[9] When Rogers became Secretary of State, he focused on human rights issues such as those after the Six-Day War in Israel. He is probably best known, according to State Department records, for his efforts to broker a lasting peace settlement between Israel and its Arab neighbors, including the Palestinian refugees. This is still a matter of first order importance— not only for Americans of Jewish and Christian heritage — but for all Americans who support democracy overseas.

Rogers accepted the Chairmanship of his alma mater's National Campaign Council at Colgate University shortly after leaving the State Department, even while he was very busy building his private law practice. I saw him up close while I served as liaison to the Council. He was gentlemanly to a fault, and insistent on getting everything done well.

Point three: The next phrase, to "establish Justice" is about installing equality under law, opportunity with accountability, and fair treatment of everyone in all circumstances. In each case, every aspect of law enforcement is to be equitably implemented. Are we doing that? For example:

- Are the civil rights of everyone, such as those guaranteed by the First Amendment, the true antecedent of the right to bear arms such as that which is indicated in the Second Amendment?
- Are violent neighborhoods actually beyond civic control?

- Is local police training adequate to protect vulnerable civilians from excessive police response?
- Are we happy as the "land of the free" to have more prisoners in jail and unfree than any other country in the world?

When the founders wrote "We the People of the United States, in order to form a more perfect Union," they followed these first words of authority and direction with the leading element of strategy for doing that: "establish Justice." Most surely they did so because they saw equity as the unbiased condition of fairness necessary to muster the voluntary participation of independent citizens in civic affairs. And that would be a first requirement of a democratic republic.

Justice is at the center of all the great faiths and the golden rule is therefore basic in all the leading religions. This comes down to the idea of the *Nth Commandment*: "Do unto others as you would have others do unto others." Always be what you want to see. Once people feel they are being treated fairly, they can focus their energies on basic tasks without fear of being harmed. This is obviously the example a President of the United States wants to set.

Howard Baker[10] was the ranking minority member of the Senate Watergate Committee who is remembered for asking about President Nixon: "What did the President know and when did he know it?" He and his colleagues epitomized the bipartisanship upon which the Constitution is predicated. When I saw him at home in Washington D.C. before hosting an address he gave at UT, he spoke of his concern about a just society. As he later said publicly, "Demography is changing us as we are older societies. We're living longer. How the generations balance each other out, how that affects education and health care" are among the most critical issues of justice. There was no question in my mind about the importance of education and health care at that time, or now.

Alam Khan is a naturalized citizen who came to America so that he could marry a woman he'd met on the Internet. He was learning to speak fluent English for a Hong Kong-based shipping company that he was working for from his home in Dhaka, Bangladesh. He is an

IT person with exceptional computer skills and homespun charm, who regularly helps me avoid technical disaster at home. He came here for opportunity and, with some struggle to be sure, he is finding it.

This is a side of justice for which America, at its best, is unequaled. "Khan," as he prefers to be called, is succeeding. But how many others, with or without his abilities, will make their way? His wife Christina, who worked as the head of the International Student Office at Colgate, where helped some two hundred fifty students from all over the world—Asia, Europe, Latin America, Africa, and the Middle East. With their savings, Khan and Christina both are helping to feed the homeless back in Dhaka where his mother regularly serves them in her home there.

Point four: The next words, to "insure domestic Tranquility," envisage our homeland as a civic sanctuary of peace where We the People enjoy the absence of fear and anxiety. Must government intrusiveness and citizen gun violence be ongoing challenges of freedom? Do we put people first or property first? Are our public spaces actually places of human dignity? Staying in power through the promotion of fear is too often primed by the scare mongering of otherwise rudderless politicians feeding off the ignorance of a frightened public. Aren't we too good for that?

After the strategic principle of establishing justice, the next principle of insuring domestic tranquility lays the groundwork for civic partnerships of every manner and purpose. To get things done, a constructive atmosphere would be necessary. And that would require attention and action on the part of all able-bodied persons.

Brad Morrice had a commitment to community well-being which was genuine even when his company's lending policies became dangerously risky. He happened to lead my first book-signing event after publication of *Leading by Heart*. This occurred several years before he, as president of New Century Financial and his colleagues in Irvine, California, set off a sub-prime mortgage debacle which helped lead to the 2008 stock market crash and the "Great Recession" which followed.[11] I am convinced that he was trying to do the right thing by reaching out to the community as was authorized by law. But the financial instruments were, contrary to what was then generally believed, fatally flawed. Sadly, that undermined the good intensions held and helped bring down the economy.

Point five: The words that "provide for the common defence" of all Americans, in partnership with allied nations, were of course intended to minimize—if not eliminate—the prospect of surprise attack by hostile nations. The fear of war was never very far from the minds of many in the new nation. That, sadly, remains true today. That fear has and does erode the bonds of trust whenever it becomes a preoccupation. When such a malaise takes hold, it erodes morale and turns healthy relationships into unhealthy wariness. Everyone suffers then, because the culture crouches, communication hesitates and commerce abates. Politics pays a price. The economy sags. Tension mounts. Prosperity weakens.

This is why an insistent inclination to diplomacy is far preferable to the wearying worry of war. Believing that war is not the best medicine isn't sufficient preparation for peace. The practice of medicine should not dominate the pursuit of health, rather what works is the other way around. The pursuit of wellness helps prevent the occurrence of illness, and eases the burden on the practice of medicine.

Peace enables prosperity even more effectively than prosperity fosters peace. It works both ways, of course, but which would you rather live with: a predominant worry or the pursuit of happiness? Wouldn't more laughter and fewer tears be better for the children? The founders seemed to be saying that a strategy of providing for the common defense follows naturally from that of insuring domestic tranquility. As citizens worked to get things done, they would likely be most productive without the worry of foreign attack. With a collectively shared responsibility for mutual security at home as well as abroad, citizens would be more confidently assured that invasive actions of any enemies would not interrupt their everyday pursuits or those peaceful pursuits of the allies with whom we trade.

W. Sterling Cole[12] was a Congressman from the Finger Lakes of Upstate New York who served as Chairman of the Joint Congressional Committee on Atomic Energy. During the second term of President Eisenhower he was tapped to be the first Director General of the International Atomic Energy Agency. Its mission was to keep America and the World safe from nuclear holocaust.

But his real challenge was to rebalance his commitment to an American strategy with an international policy that could be supported by the Soviet Union. When he later agreed to become part of Colgate's National Campaign Council headed by Secretary Rogers, I think it was because he ultimately believed that the mind must lead the muscle more effectively than the mere bluster of the beast he so often heard in the jungle of international politics. At least that was my distinct impression in listening to his personal reflections of what he thought he learned in college.

The Wall Street Journal's foreign affairs editor, Karen Elliott House,[13] earned the Pulitzer Prize for reporting on the Middle East. Immersed as she was in those entanglements, she had great concern about the U.S. being properly armed. And she let me know about that concern after kindly reading a working paper of mine at the Center for Strategic & International Studies where she was an Advisory Board member. She went on to be Publisher of the Wall Street Journal and I made some revisions in my paper to take more fully into account the fundamental role of strong military force for America's leadership in the World. That was in 1990 and my paper was about America's leadership in the midst of a world "mega-crisis." That was then. Is it much different now?

Point six: For the founders to "promote the general Welfare" in their next words, was their expression of concern to stimulate abundance for those who are able and assistance for those who are not. This would enable the good health and support for increasing productivity in the nation as a whole. Accessible healthcare, affordable education, and an emphasis on what we have come to call continuing quality improvement in every aspect of life have always seemed to be a sound formula for success. How else could the new nation be

105

productive? How else could it thrive amid uncertainties beyond control?

I suspect that the founders didn't speak about property in the Preamble not only because, as owners of property, they understood that people obviously come first, but also because slaves were considered property by delegates of the southern states whose support was necessary for ratification of the Constitution. Perhaps we consider a "social contract" of human relations before we consider a legal contract of lawful relations because "We the People" make and keep those contracts.

For the founders, promoting the general welfare seemed to be a strategy aimed at facilitating prosperity with the presence of resources for all Americans giving each the opportunity to live a life of happiness. This would apply not only to every citizen, but also to every visitor who spent more than a moment on our ground. Happiness generally makes for nicer people. Nicer people are more interested in other people's prosperity as well as their own. Prosperous people make for a safer, stronger nation of healthier communities.

John Gardner, an ex-Marine who had received the Presidential Medal of Freedom, was a hero of mine from the time in 1965 when I first read his warning about the "Anti-Leadership Vaccine" that took aim at the threat of leadership failures in higher education.[14] He was then head of the Carnegie Corporation. He became a unique national figure soon after—first as President Lyndon Johnson's Secretary of Health, Education & Welfare who helped launch Medicare—and then as the leader of Common Cause, the Urban Coalition, Independent Sector, and the Corporation for Public Broadcasting. Along the way, he authored many best-selling books on leadership in America that had a strong influence on me.

He was kind enough to make some time for me while I was at CSIS so that I could question him personally about his then current take on the state of American leadership. He was concerned that America, the democracy, was too much consumed with being America, the superpower. That was how I understood his words and philosophy.

Power follows purpose before power can lead from purpose. My words for what I believe were his thoughts. For him, thoughtfulness was preeminent. He was a leader of leaders.

Point seven is a strategic consummation of the sequential principles that lead up to it. The phrase: "and secure the Blessings of Liberty" alludes to the exercise of the inalienable rights and responsibilities of, by, and for the people. Is a good education, as Thomas Jefferson[15] and many others urged, not only essential for the conduct of democracy, but also for the requirements of a freer global world? Of course it is. How do we do that?

This consummating element of strategy about securing the Blessings of Liberty strongly suggests that a good education is part of the bottom line reality for creating and keeping the free country imagined by the founders. It is, therefore, integral to the outcome of the operating principles leading up to it. Liberty would be the basis for the fullest life possible in a unified association of citizens moving toward more rewarding futures. The outcome for all education, at its best, would need to be both a broadening and a deepening of knowledge. That would help all citizens of the republic to reach their potentials as productive people from childhood to elderhood.

Allan Cartter[16] was Chancellor of New York University, a leading economist as well as a well known leader in American higher education when I undertook a doctoral internship in his office. With his tutelage, I came to see more clearly how he saw the essence of higher education as a relationship between a student, the subject of study, and the professor. I began to see how this relationship may best be thought of as a learning partnership.

He was my doctoral advisor and a true blessing in this capstone journey. And I came to think that "partnership learning" ought to be the core thought for how a school at any level should be run. That thought would guide me all through my time at The University of Tampa. It became, for me, a reflection of how to see the world as a mighty partnership of possibilities far beyond the singular comprehension of one person alone.

That thought never seemed to leave Cartter's mind, even in his leading role at this major university. He continued advising me throughout his transition from NYU to helping Clark Kerr[17] lead the vaunted Carnegie Commission on Higher Education to its consequential conclusions for America. Caring mentors often are the most competent teachers. And competent teachers are among our most valuable citizens.

Shabbir Mansuri[18] saw the relationship of education and freedom from a different perspective. He was a Muslim from India who had settled in Southern California, and was an unusual freedom-loving educator. I knew him as a visionary leader who sought to educate Americans about the often misunderstood religion of Islam. He was the founding director of the Council on Islamic Education that has now evolved into the Council on Religion and Civic Values.

This Council has long advocated for the values shared by Jews, Christians, and Muslims that are based on the divine law of The Holy One—known to them variously as Yahweh, God and Allah. I knew Shabbir as a man of peace and an advocate of educating everyone about the Golden Rule as the prerequisite of sharing life together. This was very much in the spirit of the call to justice and tranquility found in our Preamble.

Point eight: The next following words, "to ourselves and our Posterity," carry an encompassing perspective. It runs from now to future generations and envisions a continuity and permanence of the fruits that can be harvested from seeds the current generation has planted. Infrastructure investment, for example, is perhaps the call most often heard by those most worried about the functionality of our country. They see the need to keep our infrastructure in excellent shape if we are to have a long lasting *infra-culture*—one strong enough to sustain a future of freedom.

The question, then, is how can we best sustain our prime infrastructure—the physical facilities and organizational structures necessary for the operation of a society such as the American enterprise? Aren't our schools, at every level in all fields, of paramount importance? Since ancient times the state of learning has been closely related to the state of society. Is America today a healthy and hearty learning society?

With this modification of the strategy to look at posterity and aim at supporting a sustainable future, the founders were addressing a concern that public policy avoid mere tactical advantage. They were certainly concerned about the dangers of self-dealing. They also clearly and deeply believed in the necessity of resilience and durability. And they were extra-ordinary visionaries, who saw far beyond the events of their own day to days they could hardly imagine but to which they were devoutly dedicated to serving. Are our politicians showing us that high level of statesmanship today?

Catherine Tinker[19] had a clear vision of the future as a law professor at Chapman University in California when she took the course I taught in organizational leadership. She was looking for help regarding her plan to establish an Institute on International Law & Organizations, as she called it. Catherine was a participant in the discussions at the United Nations Conference on Biodiversity in Rio de Janeiro. She had devoted much of her life to what we commonly call "sustainability." She noted that: "The costs of inaction on sustainable development with irreversible harm to ecosystems and people, are higher than the cost of actions proposed" to address it. That sums it up.

Vernon Ross was the long-time pastor of First Baptist Church in Hamilton, New York. He made his mission of ministering to kids by helping them have constructive fun. Like all the other kids he ministered to, my kids loved him. He took them fishing and canoeing; they helped him with his Christmas tree farm; they searched for old Indian arrowheads together—and occasionally even found one.

That doesn't mean that there weren't difficulties. The village kids and the farm kids didn't always mix easily. Vernon's lesson was to love life, love one another, and love your faith. He's still alive and well today, though not quite the six feet eight inches tall he was then, and the now grown-up kids always seem to have a ready hug for him when they come back home.

Point nine: In concluding their charge to the new nation, the founders thought by saying "do ordain and establish this Constitution" that they would be sanctifying its standing as the law of the land. That which is established, and also ordained, is something sacred. The founders used the term "ordain"[20] to give their launching of the Constitution a secular baptism. This was a higher calling above our everyday pre-occupations. Do we love it or do we think we are above it?

Sam Gibbons[21] was the Congressman from Tampa long before and long after my time at The University of Tampa. While I was there, UT was holding commencement exercises in both December and April. I presided at eighteen of them. Sam gave the principal address at three. He was popular in town and on campus because he seemed to embody the sanctity of America's highest callings—in effect embodying the intent of the founders in ordaining and establishing the Constitution as a living force in the work to which he devoted his life.

More specifically, he was a major voice in Congress for better education, healthcare, and world trade. When he was chairman of the Ways & Means Committee, I was asked to go to Washington and testify, because of my connection, on behalf of a federal financing plan that would assist independent colleges and universities, like The University of Tampa. So, I made my appearance, delivered our message, and answered questions. The Halls of Congress—with the public, the press, and the politicians all in evidence—were humbling. It was an experience.

Sam was a true American hero. He had parachuted behind the Nazi lines at Normandy Beach to help support the dangerous landing of the allied forces. Tom Brokaw[22] credited him with helping to inspire his best-seller on "*The Greatest Generation.*" As Sam said: "I went into politics not to win wars but to make them unnecessary." This got to the heart of his message to the people. And he never lost an election.

Point ten: After opening the Constitution and, therefore, the Preamble with the phrase—"We the People of the United States"— the founders expanded that identity in the closing words by stipulating that all the law would be "for the United States of America"—not for red states or blue states, but for the federal union in its entirety. This simple and obvious point is often forgotten by voters who do not pay close attention when politicians cover up self-interested reasons for their support of foreign nations with influential American lobbies whose interests work for their own benefit, but which may not be in the best interests of all Americans. Shameful.

Is it clear where the leadership of foreign affairs for America comes from? Does it come from the President? With the advice and consent of Congress, one way or another? What's the difference between making a law and executing it in a Constitution based on separation of powers? What is the proper role and the legitimate power of each branch of government as it involves immigrants, for example? Or, terrorism? China? World trade?

Jose Ferrer,[23] born in Puerto Rico and Anne Armstrong[24] of Texas epitomized respectfully opposite approaches to reaching Americans of different origins. I knew them separately but remember them together because they illustrate the sharp contrasts of how very different capabilities contribute importantly to leading our republic.

Ferrer was a distinguished actor, theater and film director. Always playing his roles with panache, he was the first Hispanic Oscar-winning actor for his leading role as Cyrano de Bergerac. Armstrong was a distinguished politician, diplomat, and business woman. Always communicating with directness, she was the first woman to keynote a national party convention and serve as Ambassador to the United Kingdom.

Both were board leaders of nonprofit nongovernmental organizations where I served, Jose as our actors committee chair at the Shakespeare Globe Centre of North America, and the ambassador as our board chair at the Center for Strategic & International Studies. Maybe he laughed a little more and maybe she frowned a little better, but that's who they were: one an actor and the other an ambassador. They both were outstanding American leaders.

When we look upon the top ten all together, we may get a better view of how the seed of freedom becomes the solidarity of freedom keepers, and ultimately the security of a free country. In their different ways as free people, these freedom keepers serve and protect the security of all more effectively because, in their emerging self awareness, the courage of their convictions grows, and their willingness to defend who they are is stronger. They live in the land of the free because they are brave. Do we count ourselves among the freedom keepers?

XII. LEARNING NATION

Are we a nation of learners? Free persons for a free country are, using competitive strategies, whole persons for a whole nation.

Led by a committed President and a collaborative Congress, with the Supreme Court's approval under law, our nation can open its educational doors further through civic partnerships that deliver opportunities for continuous improvement. Every organization wants its members, partners and friends to learn what is most important about it. Each has a learning system that encompasses some variation of basic tools, working knowledge, and leading ideas.

- Each considers what learning lessons are basic for all to know;
- Each manifests learning priorities in the opportunities presented and denied;
- Each supports learning standards in its expectations of achievement;
- Each determines learning access by the aid programs it underwrites.

How, then, does each do that well? What about America as a whole? How are we doing with that? Can we launch a nonpartisan competitive strategy?

When Peter Senge interviewed Ray Strata, who was the CEO of Analog Devices, he said that "the rate at which organizations learn may become the only sustainable source of competitive advantage, especially in knowledge-intensive businesses."[1] Daniel Bell, in his path-breaking writings, used the term "knowledge societies."[2] Knowledge is the resource, the multiplier of other resources, a vital part of the creative energy of action and momentum by which people go about their everyday tasks.

Learning organizations are led by systems thinkers who work with learning in systems that teach participants how to produce results effectively through those systems. And they teach their communities and customers how to use their services and products to advantage -- not just for themselves, but with and for others.

The Second Report to the Club of Rome, *Mankind at the Turning Point,* in 1974, was the principal subject in one of my UT classes. It carried a warning to the world about the multi-faceted crisis that was then brewing across the planet. Co-authors Mihajlo Mesarovic and Eduard Pestel wrote that: "It is most urgent that we do not avert our eyes from the dangers ahead, but face the challenge squarely and assess alternative paths of development in a positive and hopeful spirit."[3]

They saw "a multitude of unprecedented crises: the population crisis, the environmental crisis, the world food crisis, the energy crisis, the raw material crisis" and they saw that "the whole multitude of crises appears to constitute a single global crisis-syndrome of world development."

They saw this meta crisis "growing at an incredible speed when viewed in historical perspective" and called it the *problematique humaine*. They discussed the "organic growth" of humankind, and urged that we observe the world as a "system of interdependent and harmonious parts, each making its own unique contribution, be it in economics, resources, or culture." That perspective underlies the dictates of the Preamble and how "We the People" are entrusted to apply them in the context of a world that has grown closer and more interdependent.

Yong Zhao, an American immigrant from China, came out with an important book, *World Class Learners* in 2012,[4] that picked up on this challenge with a response aimed at "educating creative and entrepreneurial students" for such a world. It was praised by educator Diane Ravitch[5] for demonstrating that a mode of learning that helps students acquire the "freedom to think, the freedom to invent, and the freedom to differ from bureaucratically devised norms," is far more important than simply raising standardized test scores. This approach switches the focus from what is, to what is to be, while still acknowledging that they both have a role.

Zhao recently came east from the University of Oregon, where he serves as Presidential Chair for Global and Online Education to speak at the Hamilton Central School in Upstate New York. He was addressing a community audience in a place where superintendent Diana Bowers was initiating a system-wide adaptation of Zhao's concept for this small college town school district.

I was there to help her prepare for a presentation of her own concept based on the model Zhao was advocating. He argued for a new paradigm that matches child-centered learning with civic values and skills to educate productive citizens in all spheres at all levels of education.

Kids are unique, active learners who construct their own knowledge based on their personal experiences. "Children no longer live in isolated societies," Zhao explains. "They must become citizens of their local community, the nation, and also the world. That is the layered world he or she faces in order to succeed."

Learning at home has always been essential. But learning in a one-room schoolhouse is gone. Going to school doesn't have to mean going to another place. Going away to college is no longer the only way to go to college. Significant learning today occurs at different levels of intensity at home, in school, at the office, or elsewhere, and frequently on the run. Teaching is done in person, by television, on the computer or an electronic device, in a classroom, or on field trips.

Learning is done alone and in tutorials, by lecture and discussion, in seminars and workshops, in laboratories and clinics. Institutions and organizations of learning are in public and private schools. There are now for-profit learning businesses competing with public and private non-profit institutions.

Several years ago, Bob Bannister,[6] an old school chum, called to ask if I'd heard that the elementary school we had attended in Hempstead, New York, then overwhelmingly white, and now overwhelmingly brown, had been renamed in honor of President

Barack Obama,[7] reflecting the swing in the demographics of our home town.

It is now widely understood that demographics are leading the change that is unfolding for the future, even more so than technology. This is especially true when it is coupled with a commitment to educating the people. Educating the young and re-educating the generations ahead of them to keep them abreast of the ongoing changes in the world around us is even more important than the issues of war or peace; economics or politics; climate change; and the depletion of the earth's resources. Because our effective responses to all the other issues depends on how well educated and well informed we are.

The changing demographics reflect the make-up of populations and the heritage and inherited beliefs and values of people respond to everything else the world brings. With demographic change, new leaders are chosen to reflect these beliefs and values. So, We the People try to simultaneously pay attention to these changes while still holding to the continuity. And thus it is that we move forward, reaching out for the future while holding on to the past.

Cradle to grave learning—pre-school to adult school—has become a virtual necessity, as never before. Being in a constant learning mode is essential in order to have the best-educated society we can as far as the eye can see or the mind can imagine. This involves all aspects of the learning spectrum:

- Vocational, technical and professional training;
- Continuing education and lifelong learning;
- Humanities, social sciences, and the arts;
- Natural sciences, technology, engineering and mathematics;
- Learning for all ages at all times.

Knowledgeability is essential both for the individual, and for the nation. A better life depends upon what we know, what we can do, and what we value. In short, wisdom.

All of this leads to development of the whole person for the whole country. The challenge is obviously one that transcends a given locality or pursuit. Carefully synchronized learning strategies are—at local, state and national levels—to articulate an effective, economical, and efficient learning society in America. Arguments about "how" to do that are worthy, but arguments about "whether" to do that make no sense. Our lives as citizens and as a nation depend on it.

In popularizing the idea of learning organizations in his extensive writings, Peter Senge places systems thinking at the center of a mental model called the *"Fifth Discipline."* It is, in essence, a requirement for thoughtfulness in leadership of all forms and types.[8]

Systems thinking is a comprehensive way of looking at what Frederick Jervis "saw."[9] Its virtue is a holistic approach to the challenge of planning and managing that faces leadership. It follows all the way from a vision of the future to the velocity of getting there. It requires big picture focus, simplification of the complexities involved, and creating unified support of the mission. If we do that, we are golden, and we can all have a hand in the rule.

For a learning organization to work, its members must take responsibility for its success. Some say there is no "I" in team. The "I" is there, though that is not what we see first. Rather what we see first is the whole team, with a certain identity in form and substance. Individuals, whom we then see, are partners of other individuals in order to get complex tasks accomplished.

As they come together, individuals become team members—partners who learn together in the overall individual learning process. The synergy that becomes possible with interpersonal learning can be exciting and productive. We, as a society, need people, organizations, and systems of all kinds to work at optimal levels— both for their own sake and ours.

Philip Howard[10] is founder and Chair of Common Good, an organization that examines the way the American government operates under the law when it purports to take care of the business of the people. In the *Rule of Nobody*,[11] he explains how we are tied up in legal knots by judges, politicians and bureaucrats some of whom have long since gone from the scene, and some of whom are still hard at work, but leaving us with an impossible legacy. Howard urges us to untie the knots and take responsibility for reclaiming this loss of leadership caused by legalisms and replace the situation with a new leadership ethic of more principled decision-making by accountable officials.

Howard councils that: "fixing democracy is a moral imperative for citizens, not just public officials." New choices need to be made. Therefore, new knowledge needs to be brought to the table everywhere that governing bodies convene to decide on matters of public business. "The old vision of human responsibility," Howard said, should be "the new vision of government"—moved more constructively, I would add, by the new leadership ethic. Having knowledge is one thing. Using it is another. And using it well, for the public benefit, is still another.

American statistician and consultant W. Edwards Deming,[12] a pioneer of quality management, relentlessly aimed at the continuous improvement of the operating systems that govern how an organization works. He insisted that "a bad system will beat a good person every time." That may not be the whole story, but it sums up the main story all too well. He was best known for his work with the leaders of Japanese industry after World War II, and was widely considered to have been the catalyst of Japan's catapult to world leadership in manufacturing because he insisted on finely tuned systems.

His leadership theory was based on what he called a "system of profound knowledge," which featured an appreciation of the system's nature, an understanding of the variations likely to affect its efficiency, the limits of what can be known about its administration, and the role of human nature, inherited and acquired, in running it. The highest value was placed on the education and training of the responsible participants. They were all considered partners in the enterprise and it was then recognized that their shared efforts made the difference. It worked wonders.

In Washington, and in the halls of government everywhere in America, consensus-building is a necessity for government to work. In the democratic process, there are majorities who set the agenda and there are minorities in loyal—but not obstructive—opposition. The job is to create a dialogue where each side can talk to the other about their interests and differences, and then seek avenues for mutual gain without shutting down the work of government—the business of the People. This is "Democracy 101," as we might say of a college course.

Yet the widely respected scholars studying Congress today, Thomas Mann and Norman Ornstein,[13] have observed that this "dialogue" is not happening now in Washington where a small minority of members have been flunking Democracy 101. Stalemate has been the order of the day and individual interest in getting re-elected is trumping the job of working to promote the values set forth in the Preamble.

In this situation, the seed of freedom is blown away in the wind, the solidarity of the People is damaged in the storm, and the security of America is threatened in the aftermath. The Constitution is built on the expectation that lawmakers would function collectively for the people of the republic. Are we now, finally, learning that bipartisanship for America is the better way?

XIII. AMERICAN PRAGMATISM

Not political expediency? The opposite: opening paths to a moral excellence of respect, for mutual prosperity.

Being pragmatic is not about being politically expedient. Rather, it is about engaging collective results. Could it, contrary to popular thought, produce a path to moral excellence? Could we imagine that freedom is an outcome of respect for mutuality that leads to prosperity? Could we imagine that unfreedom can be an outcome of disrespect for others that can lead to poverty? And then, as Ghandi said, that poverty can lead to violence?[1] Hard to believe?

Pragmatism lies at the heart of the American idea. It is actually America's distinct contribution to world philosophy. It comes, at least in part, from the daunting call of the Preamble to the awesome responsibilities of freedom—from the soul, to the solidarity, and then the security of the nation.

Pragmatism is really about doing what works for the people. Think of it as working to achieve the greatest good of the People, for the largest number by the People, over the longest period for the People, at the lowest cost to the People. This is what the founders thought the vision set forth in the Preamble would do — one way or another. This is what would be, in essence, a new leadership ethic—because we haven't lived up to the expectations of the old one—which I believe is inherent in the reasoning of the Preamble.

This basis of how the Founders envisioned the new nation would operate—by and for "We the People"—seems largely to have been overlooked. But I believe the Pope would agree with the founders' intent. After all, we don't have to choose between values and practicalities, but we do have to balance them. As the Pope said to Congress: "Let us seek for others the same possibilities which we seek for ourselves. In a word, if we want security, let us give security; if we want life, let us give life; if we want opportunities, let us provide opportunities. The yardstick we use for others is the yardstick which time uses for us."[2] This is a profound truth we often forget.

Pragmatism is actually the opposite of the political expediency many have mistaken it to be. Its most basic concern is about learning from the collective experience to facilitate the general well-being, and not to deal with just the exigencies of immediate circumstance. Pragmatism arises from the moral order of interdependence and grows into the practical order of personal experience. It is not the other way around.

Noam Chomsky, professor of linguistics at MIT, was discussing the Israeli-Palestinian conflict when he quoted the former head of Israel's General Security Service as saying that "those who want victory against terror without addressing underlying grievances want an unending war." He also quoted the former head of Israeli Military Intelligence as saying "Those who hope for mutual survival for the Arabs must accept a minimum of respect for Arab society. The alternative is unending war."[3] And the Wall Street Journal found, after 9-11, that "moneyed Muslims" supported U.S. policies in general, but hated its support for corrupt regimes that undermined their democratic development.[4]

Pragmatism, not personal or political expediency, is what William James strongly believed in and what he persuasively addressed for many years. His was one of many interpretations of "American Pragmatism."[5] But, he was one of its originators, a founder of psychology as a discipline of learning, and a leading American intellectual of his generation who became pragmatism's primary spokesman.

In his 1906 speech at Stanford University, James argued for "the moral equivalent of war"[6] which would provide political unity in pursuit of civic virtue for the cause of freedom. But, is this possible? We seem to think so. Is freedom not necessary for survival?

As he saw it, this would link patriotic duty with human decency in some form of national service by all American youth as they come of age. This duty would be civilian in nature, and only of a military

121

nature as it had to be. The alms of compassion would be pointedly preferred to the armaments of killing. The latter would routinely be reserved only for times of emergency. Whatever the form of service, every young American would submit to a disciplined experience of work for the country and its cause of freedom.

Every young citizen, then, in coming of age, would learn by doing what it takes to be an American. This would encompass looking out for your mates while you're looking out for yourself; taking care of others while taking care of yourself; cleaning up the act of others while you are cleaning up yourself; and giving what you've got in exchange for getting what you give.

This opportunity would enable those entering maturity to experience the great law of reciprocity[7] and the balancing scale of justice. If they learn that, then never again would it be forgotten that we owe our lives to others before we can then live our own lives. This would teach those involved to know that a nation is nothing if it is not first its people. And, then, a nation is everything when it becomes — at the same time — "of, by, and for" all its people.

The great sin in such a nation is selfishness which is slavery to oneself. The great service is selflessness which is freedom from oneself. These are the reality twins of the great and the small. Their lives are renewed and uplifted as the sun shines equally on everyone and especially on anyone who stands before its light and gives thanks.

Let us explore the use of power in governance. Are the people being empowered to take control of their decisions, and to do so wisely? Power is neutral. Its effects depend on how it is used. It can be used for good or evil. It can be moral or immoral. It can result in the right thing or the wrong thing. If people come first, as the Preamble mandates, then their empowerment is the precondition of social and civic life—that is good, moral and right.

This is precisely what has not happened politically in most of the country. Empowerment is unfortunately not predominant in the inner cities of our metropolitan areas. It also is not predominant in rural outreaches of the countryside. Under such conditions of disempowerment, it would be "impossible for a youth who is a member of a group which is powerless in the community to grow to maturity without some trauma to his perception of himself because of the compromised position of his group in communal life."[8]

This is the view of Dan W. Dodson, late professor of sociology at New York University and chairman of the board of the former Council for American Unity on which he served with baseball's Jackie Robinson. He went on to observe that: "Our urban youth are characterized by mass apathy with its attendant low aspiration levels, and sense of individual alienation and lack of worth."

Although much as been done *for* these youth, it has not been done *with* them. Real partnerships have been in little evidence. Power sharing has not been a comprehensive and sustaining part of the problem solving. People have not been engaged in creating what they get. Rather they have been told what they are getting.

"We the People," therefore, have not been part owners of the solutions. Those in power have treated many of our citizens as people who are incapable of being part of this ownership. So they have become, in effect, dependents and been considered free loaders, because that is the way they have been treated. That is unhealthy from virtually every standpoint. Problem unsolved. Then, those with no responsibility for the solutions feel less responsibility for enforcing them.

Abraham Lincoln was a devout man. His devotion was not because he went to church, but because he believed in and said his prayers. His devotion was not because he professed his beliefs, but because he lived his life as he believed. His devotion was not because he did his part but because he loved the whole. He gave his life and he saved a nation. America is free because he served.

What we need to imagine now is what we should do to make America's mission, set forth in our "Preamble of Freedom," a reality for our country, for ourselves, and for the generations to come. And then we would need to be unswerving in our pursuit of it. We must back plan the all-important details, as Frederick Jervis would have said, and then lead forward to implement them for the future of America and for the rest of the world. In doing so, we can set an ongoing example and help it to thrive.

We are now in the Post-Industrial Age driven by the soft power of knowledge. The fabled Industrial Age was driven by the hard power of machines. We have gone from hand technology to head technology to high technology. The old hardware has been transcended by the new software. This not only has put brains before brawn, but also heart beforehand.

When Warren Buffett recently summed up what others have said before—"the more you learn the more you earn"—he wasn't talking just about money. He was talking about investing in yourself as a person so that you will be better able "to build strong relationships and partnerships to be successful." He believed that "great partnerships make any job easier." And you will enjoy it so much "you will never work a day in your life."[9]

I never did meet Peter Drucker.[10] But I did talk with him on the phone. I asked him to speak at a Chapman University conference I was organizing because I could think of no one better for our purposes. He had one word for me: "No." He was almost ninety and he was a star at nearby Claremont Graduate University in southern California. We shared a strong belief in the importance of nonprofit organizations for the future of a free society. But he didn't travel any longer. So, "good luck, and thank you for calling."

That was disappointing. Dr. Drucker was one of the great modern minds of American business. I'd read much of his stuff. I met some of his disciples and admired the way he lived. He liked to advise people that we are in a "Post-Capitalist Society." Capital is a means, not the end. If you want to make money, you must invest in people first. We do well to remember that. Another great American who was born elsewhere—in Austria—and helped everwhere—across the modern world.

We have learned that our emotions organize our thoughts, not the other way around. Drucker seemed to have an intuitive feel for that. Skills and innovation are driven by values and ethics. Soft power leads the hard choices. You may be more left than right brained or more right brained than left brained. Of course, you have only one brain which integrates both hemispheres along with the strengths of each. Whatever that combination may be, it is a balance of their energy that works.

"Higher education is America's best industry," contends another notable immigrant, Fareed Zakaria, who grew up in India. "With 5 percent of the world's population, the United States absolutely dominates higher education." He observed that "in the industrial age, hardware mattered; today it is software also known as 'culture.' This" he said, " is a grab bag of skills, openness."[11]

Leadership rests on a pragmatic knowledge of how relationships work. The moral imperative is to get that right. So, the question is: how does the creative drive work? This is the *Drive* of our energy; the *Nuclear* mass from which we grow; and the *Acceleration* of speed with which our light beam—our vision—travels, the organizing DNA, our ODNA as a nation.[12]

The light beam of America is our vision of freedom. How are we doing with that? When any light beam is leading us best, to paraphrase the ancient Chinese philosopher Lao Tzu,[13] the people will barely know how. And when it is done, its aim fulfilled, they will think that they did it themselves. History tells us it usually works that way. Trouble is, we don't seem to realize that. A shame.

Freedom is paradoxical. It requires submission. It entails responsibility. It must produce moral, social, cultural and civic order. Or it dies. We fight for freedom mentally to keep it materially or it will not work. Freedom, therefore, is a strategy to which we commit, or it is nothing but an ideal unconsummated. So, too, is the commitment that is required to fulfill the ideals and promises of the Preamble and of the Constitution itself.

Edward Luttwak,[14] a distinguished military strategist at the Center for Strategic & International Studies, long argued for what he called the "paradoxical logic" of a strategy that supports the idea that you must prepare for war if you want peace. This may be more reassuring to those focused on fighting evil and less so to those focused on doing good.

If we follow the logic of William James' argument,[15] we would prepare for the worst while pursuing the best. The challenge would then be how to prioritize the advancements of humankind that become possible in times of peace without neglecting the preparations that become necessary in case of war.

Our response to that challenge requires serious attention to the bad while we concentrate primarily on the good. The logic of that argues for a practical, level-headed approach to the future which would embrace the potential of peace differently than we might think.

Peace, then, would be less the outcome of happiness and more the result of hopefulness. Happiness is a state of being and hopefulness is more a state of expectation. While both are nice, expectation may be more inclined to action. And action is a necessity.

Because the world is a place where good and evil coexist, to realize the first we must outsmart the second, not ignore it. This, at least, is the conclusion that meets the pragmatic standards of logic and simplicity which I had the privilege of considering in digesting Luttwak's work, listening to his discussions with other strategists, and engaging him in personal conversation at CSIS. For me, eye opening.

The instruments for getting around the law are excesses of wealth, ideology, and power itself. These excesses are examples of boldfaced expediency, not beneficent pragmatism. Power, in these cases, is consolidated in the hands of a few to serve the fever of their compulsions. They take power from the many to serve themselves individually—sadly intolerable for the future of the nation.

In looking at both civic engagement and military strategy, one invariably finds that human capital comes first. But we must be very careful how we use it. There simply is no way around the differences between the people who are the receivers of funding, the objects which the funding pays for, and the distributors who provide the funding in the first place.

Thus, an "iron triangle" is created among a bureaucracy, congressmen, and lobbyists that results in the mutual benefit of all three. Human capital, financial capital and political capital become intermingled in a web of selfish influence sunk below the horizons of civic virtue.[16] We must not forget this iron triangle as we argue about our differences. And we must find ways to safeguard the public interest from the shameful excesses.

Think back to what Adam Smith, the founder of capitalism, actually had to say about people and property in his works.[17] Smith made a more thoughtful argument than he is given credit for. His point was, in essence, that moral sentiments are the flip side of practical pursuits. They are partners even as they present choices. One comes with the other. Two sides of the same coin, again. Smith emphasized individual initiatives and—we often forget—he embraced their moral considerations.

Just as the principles upon which America was founded are those of classic republicanism, the practices at the heart of our modern republic are those of democratic capitalism. Smith knew very well that moral sentiments could not be left out of the equation. He emphasized that they be exercised at the initiative of entrepreneurs. This is the heart of all enterprise. But, capitalism has been bent out of shape by self-seeking shape shifters.

Pope Francis has picked up on this.[18] He has attacked capitalists for their misuse of capitalism to fatten their pocketbooks at the expense of the people. The poor are being defunded by the rich. The rich are using their power to keep the poor in their place, so the rich can continue to exploit them. Of course, there are some magnificent exceptions, but not nearly enough. That has to change. Healthy capitalism is essential for "the general Welfare."

Some of the Pope's detractors have accused President Barack Obama of being "the Pope's President" because they have favored similar policies to address this malingering situation. Do those who think the President is not a Christian think he is acting too Catholic?

Whatever one's point of view, it is hard to see how one's political views can be entirely separate from one's religious views. President Kennedy, for one, dealt with this conundrum. Of course these are different spheres of thought. But we like to say that all thoughts come from hearts and minds, don't we?

New research is showing that our emotions come first—they precede our capacity to reason. They organize our thoughts. Our thoughts arise from our emotions. In other words, we can't separate them, but we can, and must, respect their complementary functions. We need them both in good working order.

Whoever is pope, and whoever is president, isn't the moral imperative to keep the freedom of religious discourse from interfering with the freedom of political discourse with one actually reinforcing, not undercutting, the other? Moral authority, which is behind all political legitimacy, is dependent on our respect for the truth, as best we can ascertain it. R-E-S-P-E-C-T, sang Aretha Franklin.[19]

On the road from Jerusalem to Jericho, so the biblical story goes, a Samaritan ministered to a man who had been beaten and robbed by thieves. As he lay in plain sight alongside the road, two strangers had passed him by without helping. One of the strangers was a priest, the other a citizen. They showed him no compassion although they should have known, according to the prophet Micah, what was considered to be right action according to the law of the time: "to act justly and to love mercy and to walk humbly with your God."[20]

The Samaritan, a person of lower class, saw by the road only one of God's children, in dire need of assistance. This "Good Samaritan" assisted that person, dressed the man's wounds, took him to a nearby inn for healing, and provided for his recovery. The Samaritan was a man who actually followed this law of the prophets even though he was a man shunned by the others. It was he who showed mercy. People are advised to "go and do likewise." That is the law of the prophets.

Sari Nusseibeh[21] had an improbable task as President of Al-Quds University when I met him during a visit he made to California. A group of sympathetic friends in America, that was led by his American representative, Rabia Husseini, the widow of his predecessor, were struggling to raise funds for this "Arab University of Jerusalem," as it was known.[22]

But America's pre-occupation with Israel and the contentious politics of Jerusalem led to hesitancy on the part of many prosperous Palestinian Americans to become actively engaged in the project. I witnessed these efforts first hand for several testy years, while serving as a consultant to the project. It was inspiring, but disappointing. This was and is a noble cause which, for me after the loss of my brother at the alleged hands of Palestinian terrorists, was close to my heart. These good Palestinian expatriates were not pragmatic in the fullest sense of that term because they could hardly be. They were demoralized and hesitant to invest their personal resources.

Lifelong learning for any peoples who aspire to create and sustain a nation that works for the benefit and viability of its people is essential. This is true whether it relates to the education of Americans, or anyone else. Thus, the education of Palestinians is essential for the ultimate sustainability of that population as a viable people. America's higher education is one of our greatest strengths. What we want for ourselves, we must also want for others. That is the *Nth commandment*. That is the ultimate dealmaker. To do otherwise is the inevitable deal breaker.

When we spread our seed of freedom, we grow our solidarity as a people and strengthen our security in America. We also strengthen those around the world who love the idea of freedom and can imagine the creative advantages it has for them as they are able to adapt it to their own situations.

Not long ago, in a television interview with Charlie Rose, Russian President Vladimir Putin responded to a question about what he thought of America. His answer was that he admired its creativity. This has long been America's great strength, leading to the political and economic power of the nation. We must pay more attention to that creativity. It comes with freedom.

XIV. MENTAL MAPS

Is thoughtfulness a productive asset? Yes because it takes both minds and hearts to find where we want to go together.

Mental dynamics and moral bandwidth lead to thoughtfulness. Thoughtfulness isn't a term that is normally used in global politics. Yet it is precisely the ever present state that we should focus on because it draws upon the full treasure of minds and hearts that are the targets of the messages we send. The receivers of these messages react. Thoughtfulness, at its best, does not leave out any consideration that is likely to spark a desired reaction. It includes all possibilities for reaching a desired result, and cares for the way it may play out on the world stage. Thoughtfulness, in short, wants to optimize impact—the core of the "new leadership ethic."

Is thoughtfulness, therefore, basic to leading a continental nation? When we are pragmatic, we have significant concern for the cognitive metabolism or mental agility of our fellow Americans. Cognitive metabolism is about the ability to think well. When fully functioning, this ability engages our mental dynamics and our moral bandwidth with each other. Both are needed simultaneously at center stage in the American psyche—again, the two sides of a coin. To get the return on the investment necessary for the pursuit of freedom, we must give strong support to the essential elements of such thoughtfulness, both at home and abroad, while keeping our commitments in balance with our budgets.

Oliver Sacks[1] was a neurologist who became well known for his authorship of *The Man Who Mistook His Wife for a Hat.* He found that many of the catatonic patients he saw had become locked inside themselves as a result of what he called their "sleeping sickness." He gave them a drug called L-dopa and watched as they "emerged into a world they didn't recognize." I wonder if Americans today are still struggling to awaken from their own political sleeping sickness via some occasional catatonic fits of anger? How else may we explain such frequent reports of outrage and violence as are visited upon us today?

131

Jeffrey Lieberman has written about "wraparound" services for adolescents and young adults with symptoms of psychotic disorders that might endanger others if left untreated.[2] He noted the urgency of access to professional diagnosis where "pharmacological, psychological, educational and social-support treatments can engage patients in recovery." These are now becoming available in my home state of New York, but we must hasten to develop and utilize specialized centers that are emerging across the country. Now, we need to be talking about a wraparound strategy for addressing the political sleeping sickness which afflicts us.

Lieberman went on to say that such centers ought to be complexes that provide "medical management, psychotherapy, rehabilitation services and supervised residential facilities." And they ought not be blocked by those who don't want treatment to be legally required for mental disorders as they are for tuberculosis or sexually-transmitted diseases. These centers and the treatment they provide could help greatly to reduce the violent killings that are now so troubling America.

However, political sleeping sickness is more than anything else, an educational challenge. Schooling that is engaging, that induces pro-active learning, that goes deep and wide into subjects, that deals with the requisite skill sets, is a primary factor. Communities that are friendly and open and supportive are essential. Attention from those of abundance to those needing assistance needs to become normal.

Barbara Sloop[3] retired as a Captain in the U.S. Public Health Service (PHS) where, in her final years, she worked for and often rode to work with then U.S. Surgeon General Everett Koop[4] who lived nearby. Though it was not part of her professional portfolio, her vantage point at the National Institutes of Health gave her a close view of what was happening with the mental health patients discharged from institutional care as the federal government cut budgets which supported them. And she was appalled.

Barbara is my cousin, and after her retirement from PHS, she continued her care for people as an ordained pastor who still spends much of her time with people who are afflicted with combinations of spiritual, mental and physical difficulties. But church-based efforts such as hers simply cannot do enough. Our nation sorely needs to place the mental health of all our citizens among the topmost priorities of national policy.

As we do so, we will not escape the powerful economic drivers that will pave the way forward as our leaders search for the right directions in which to move. When leaders and participants take the route of thoughtfulness to heart, it will become clearer what should be held in mind and faithfully followed. When it comes to planning and managing budgets, it becomes clearer about what constitutes the best return on investment of precious resources.

So, in identifying both expenditure and income expectations that are most likely to affect those desired program outcomes, our first attention is to provide for efficiency. This is not a comfortable thought for many who think of it as a version of cheap. No. Efficiency in resource use always is a balance of effectiveness and economy, doing the greatest good in the least costly way. And efficiency is never perfect.

What's more, balanced thinking helps make balanced budgets. So, we strive for balanced judgments in the public mind. This is essential for everything else to succeed. Without this priority, it is an uphill battle to get beyond the myriad complex problems that break out, often unpredictably and usually at a significant cost to national well being. And budget balancing is the bottom line we always face. Not the top priority, of course, but the bottom line of necessity.

This is where the Preamble comes back into the picture. When we consider "We the People...in Order to form a more perfect Union...and secure the Blessings of Liberty," we encounter what we could profitably take as a warning. To wit: We the People must be able and willing to act responsibly for the common good of all Americans if the Preamble is going to be the living spirit of America. In looking at the priorities, then, when it comes to budgeting resources, the interests of all the people need to be factored in. We haven't reached the bottom line until that is done.

There is no security without solidarity. Otherwise people fall through the social net, disappear into the darkness, and come out shooting— from the mouth or the barrel of a gun or both.

In his address to Congress, Pope Francis said that "It goes without saying that part of this great effort is the creation and distribution of wealth. The right use of natural resources, the proper application of technology and the harnessing of the spirit of enterprise are essential elements of an economy which seeks to be modern, inclusive and sustainable."[5] Amen.

Hank Greenberg was the board of trustees leader with whom I worked most closely at CSIS in my role as chief development officer. He was chair of the board committee on development. And he had a grandly pragmatic view of the powers on Wall Street and in Washington that was global in its sweep. He had a consuming interest in the service industry he represented which, as he saw it, was severely underrepresented in the halls of Washington.

He had a good vantage point, since he led the largest insurance company in the world, and was looking for all the federal co-operation he could get. Greenberg was already one of the wealthiest men in America. He thought his association with CSIS could help him achieve the greater leadership role he envisioned for his business interests which he saw as coinciding with America's public interests. Thus, the country would benefit and so would he, along with his Wall Street partners and friends.

All of that left no doubt why he had become such a leading part of CSIS's development program which played a role in its leadership among think tanks in the defense and foreign policy world. His leadership had made AIG not only the world's largest insurance company, but also one of Wall Street's most influential powers. In the crash of U.S. stock market in 2008, AIG received the biggest U.S. government bailout of the "too big to fail" institutions. He was also subject to a civil suit for fraud and forced to leave AIG. At ninety years old, he is still nimble, staying fit, deeply involved with politics, and fighting the charges.[6]

Tom Donohue,[7] an old friend from my college development days, is the long-serving CEO of the U.S. Chamber of Commerce, the largest pro-business advocacy group in Washington. When I was at CSIS and he was at the American Trucking Association, I would fly up from Washington on his corporate jet for Board meetings of the American Management Association's Operation Enterprise that taught high school and college kids about management and leadership.

Tom was an upfront guy and a successful lobbyist. He knew the Presidents well as he served the interests of his powerful business constituents well. But, how well do the interests of his constituents, or any other special interests, match up with the interests of the American public? As with any other special interest lobby, the answer to that can best be sifted out and argued on the basis of the Preamble's litmus test. I am sure Tom would agree.

Frederick Jervis asked, as so many others do when it comes to lobbyists, who benefits at what cost? How do the benefits for those who reap them compare with their effects on the general Welfare? How does the greater good weigh in the equation? These questions must be asked by the People, picked up by the media, and passed on to the public officials who have responsibility.

John Naisbitt[8] had an impressive run as a thinker, writer and speaker in the run-up to the year 2000. As a member of the Florida Governor's Council of 100 in the early 1980's, I got an advance hearing of the trademark address which he expanded into his best-selling book *Megatrends*. Soon after that talk, I got to chat with him when he came to speak at The University of Tampa. John saw us as living in a "time of parenthesis, the time between eras." He believed that: "Those who are willing to handle the ambiguity of this in-between period and anticipate the new era will be a quantum leap ahead of those who hold on to the past." This is still very true.

So, it is a time for questioning our priorities and for capitalizing on the mind power—the quantum leap potential—that continues the inimitable advance of technology into the future. In the end, "we have extraordinary leverage and influence," Naisbitt says: "if we can only get a clear sense, a clear conception, a clear vision, of the road ahead." And, I would add, we have the core of that vision in the Preamble.

Naisbitt's mantra was about sailing with the wind—the wind that blows with the force of freedom and creativity and that leads to a future of abundance. John was always excited. He was looking ahead. That is what Frederick Jervis emphasized, looking forward—after planning backwards from a vision in order to manage toward it more aggressively —and this is exactly what our founders did in the Preamble.

The momentum of America depends upon the rediscovery of the landmark significance of our national purpose for the world. It is inscribed in the opening words of the first written constitution in the history of the world: the U.S. Constitution. That document "secures the Blessings of Liberty to ourselves and our Posterity" as authorized by "We the People of the United States, in order to form a more perfect Union," which required them to "establish Justice, insure domestic Tranquility, provide for the common defence, [and] promote the general Welfare". It's our DNA. These are the organizing principles that "ordain and establish this Constitution for the United States of America."

Look at it this way. The Preamble actually lays out the elements of America's DNA in a handy format. "We the People" is the lifestream which is forming "a more perfect Union"—as the *Drive*—which equates to and is made possible by how well the people establish a system of "Justice" that "insures domestic Tranquility" and a core of supporters who "provide for the common defence" and "promote the general Welfare"—as the *Nucleus*—that would "secure the Blessings of Liberty to ourselves and our Posterity"—as the *Accelerator*. This, in a nutshell, is how the freedom meta force of America's DNA works.

Bob Martinez was the mayor of Tampa during most of my years at the University there.[9] He epitomized the DNA of both the city and of the University—how things seemed to work. He was an active trustee, a generous supporter, and a good friend. He helped us revitalize the city-owned river front park that bordered our campus, located the city's public access television studios at the University, sponsored the installation of an Olympic track around the soccer field in our new stadium, supported the upgrade of our historic museum, and more, behind the scenes.

One evening when I was chauffeuring him and his wife Mary Anne to an important event for which we were late, I had exited out of a side street in heavy traffic and was pulled over by a police officer for "endangerment". After a few long minutes, and while the officer was checking my license, the mayor decided to see what was going on and stepped out of the car. He asked if a ticket was to be issued. "Oh no sir, no sir," said the officer. The mayor got back in the car and we drove away. No favors asked. That's the way it was. For better or worse, good friends in high places sometimes mean a lot. Friends are friends. It depends upon what we expect in our friendships.

The Mayor went on to serve as Governor of Florida and U.S. "Drug Czar" for President George H.W. Bush. He was a pragmatist. And he was, for me, an illustration of how our American system works. Access is crucial to action, and attention is necessary for access. That is fundamental in a republic of democracy. It comes down to how we get that attention and how it is used. Sometimes you must take the risk of driving into heavy traffic.

"A good political leader," Pope Francis said to Congress, "is one who, with the interests of all in mind, seizes the moment in a spirit of openness and pragmatism. A good political leader always opts to initiate processes rather than possessing spaces."[10]

Mental agility or thoughtfulness, the physical dynamics and the moral bandwidth together, are more than simply an individual characteristic. They can avert political sleeping sickness. They are very much part of a political sub-culture that greatly influences how a body politic works, whether it is local or national. Our challenge in America is how to steer the processes that the Pope spoke of in such a way that they add to the meaning of freedom for all.

XV. ACCOUNTABLE NOW

An immigrant's accounting tool? We think of Albert Einstein as a great scientist. But he was also our uncertified public accountant.

The Preamble is America's accountability tool. A magnificent coincidence of any distillation of the Preamble, such as the one we are considering, is its synchronicity with that most famous of all accounting tools—although we don't think of it that way— the one discovered by another American immigrant, Albert Einstein. This, of course, is the equation we've all heard about, don't know much about, then virtually never think about: $E=mc^2$. If we pause for a moment to consider it, we will see that it is all about just three things: energy, mass, and light. Everything we learn about lives and dies according to its rules. The same is true with the Preamble, at least for Americans.

Einstein's formula was dramatically summarized by best-selling author, Brian Greene back in 2005 on the hundredth anniversary of Einstein's discovery, when he observed that: "There is nothing you can do, not a move you can make, not a thought you can have, that doesn't tap directly into $E=mc^2$. Einstein's equation is constantly at work, providing an unseen hand that shapes the world into its familiar form."[1]

This accounting tool of the universe came from a German refugee who had fled Nazi persecution and then accepted an appointment at the Institute for Advanced Study in Princeton where he continued his work while reaching a world-wide audience. For Albert Einstein, the tool we now know as $E=mc^2$ would keep the books of the universe in balance—making him, after a fashion, the universe's uncertified public accountant. He discovered it long before he came to America, but he came to America in order to continue pursuing the explorations that his genius had opened up.

This equation, of course, is not something any of us currently use in our day-to-day life. But, maybe we should. It demonstrates that everything consists of energy—both *potential energy* available for use at any given moment which is equivalent to and balanced by *kinetic energy*, or the mass into which it may be converted at the velocity of light—which is the speed and direction of its radiation from the sun. It may seem strange, but it is a big deal. Here's why.

Everything that exists is created this way, including you and me. The maximum velocity of light, which is transposed as our vision, is bent—slowed—as it is attracted by whatever gravitational pull may affect it along the way. In the case of the earth, that pull would be the sun which—by the chemical elements contained in its light—creates us, then leads and feeds us.

In the case of the equations that relate to us as the earth's people, that pull would be whatever and whoever leads us and feeds us. This makes it very important how leadership works and how it is held accountable. Leadership is the pulling power that attracts us toward its source.

The world would, therefore, be created or destroyed according to this rule of conversion—the big bang works either way. This, no doubt, is why the famous equation has been called the "most important scientific icon of the modern era." And the organizational DNA of "We the People" in America happens to correspond with it. The Drive of DNA equates to the E or Energy of $E=mc^2$. The Nucleus of DNA equates to the m or mass of $E=mc^2$. And the Acceleration of DNA equates to the c^2 or velocity of light in $E=mc^2$. Through this understanding, human learning continues to evolve and the human race continuously adapts.

Only since the advent of modern science, from the time of Galileo and Newton,[2] has learning begun to employ systematic means of investigation and analysis along with the synthesis and verification of findings. And these findings would always be subject to further questioning and correction. Einstein's energy-mass equivalence has stood the test of time and appears to be the deep base from which we may compare our growth potential with its sustainable development.

Einstein's discovery may, therefore, be thought of as the great equivalency translator of our lives in that it balances our potential energy with our prospective use of it. If these are not equivalent, they are out of balance. This would be true whether the equation was accounting for the creation of resources or for their destruction. Either way, Einstein. In a time of urgency, the question would be about how, as they say in Washington, to "crisis manage" the balance.

Just like the earth is pulled round the sun by the force of the sun's all-powerful gravity, so does the creative drive of energy from any source lead to a nucleus of critical mass that accelerates around that source, always at the speed of light squared. We are, in essence, where we came from, subject of course to circumstances.

This is why circles of influence work. Like the weather, they work in spirals of attraction. This is how our DNA works, over and over as it grows and evolves and finds its way ahead. Whether it is for better or for worse is up to us.

Brian Greene's statement that "there is nothing you can do that doesn't tap directly into $E=mc^2$," gets across the most important point which is that $E=mc^2$, in computer lingo, is the "creative program" that all action follows on its way to making things happen, for good or ill. It refers to the energy that drives us, the mass that grows us, and the light that beams us on our way.[3]

Sir James Jeans,[4] British physicist and mathematician, who was a friend of Einstein's and a distant cousin of Bobbie's, once said that, given the universe as we describe it, "God must be a mathematician." He also said: "The human race had inhabited the earth for hundreds of thousands of years. Until the last few hundred years most people thought the earth was flat, and a few misguided people still think it is." Jeans, too, was a genius.

Learning is about faithfully pursuing truth, and in doing so, discarding false impressions that no longer hold. This is what knowing is about, and this is what Sir James was talking about. Knowledge is power. More knowledge is usually better than less, provided of course that we come to some reasonable understanding of it, which is wisdom.

And while we are at it, let's not forget the lamentation of T.S. Eliot. "Where is the knowledge we have lost in information?" he cried.[5] We are swamped with information. What does it all mean? Until we know how to decipher it, the information is pretty much meaningless and of little use. So, we are faced with the task of making sense of it. And this leads us back to knowing, as best we can, what we are doing. Again, wisdom.

Those who work in and have control over the public media have a very great responsibility to report the facts of a story as they honestly see them, and to comment fairly on those facts as they actually understand them. In their reports and commentary, they are accountable for making the whole story clear. The whole story is described by the answers to a few necessary questions I learned about during a grade school newspaper field trip to the Columbia University Graduate School of Journalism in New York City— "who, what, when, where, why, how?"

Whatever is said about the alleged facts, they must be reported as clearly as circumstances permit, would we not agree? The follow-up question then would be to understand just what it is that is actually said. Is it a report of the facts or a commentary about the facts? That's why the most respected and widely-read newspapers separate the news from the editorials. That guarantees nothing. But it does help us understand the meaning of what is being said. And that is most important. To ask what happened is to ask what it means, not just what is said.

Alexander Hamilton, perhaps our most famous immigrant, was George Washington's aid-de-camp, the first U.S. Treasury Secretary, and the subject of a must-see musical hit now playing on Broadway. He was also a prolific writer. After the drafting of the Constitution, in The Federalist No. 70, he alluded to the potential of energy—as later prescribed in Einstein's equation —especially as it pertains to matters of higher moment, as being of highest importance. He said specifically:

> *"Energy in the Executive is a leading character in the definition of good government. It is essential to the*

141

protection of the community against foreign attacks; it is not less essential to the steady administration of the laws; to protection of property against those irregular and high-handed combinations which sometimes interrupt the ordinary course of justice; to the security of liberty against the enterprises and assaults of ambition, of faction, and of anarchy."[6]

Whether one was a federalist or an anti-federalist at that time, it was clear that Hamilton was arguing for a well-led national government. He went on to say, simply, "that unity is conducive to energy will not be disputed."[7]That was his conclusion. Political persuasions aside, that is indisputable. Unity is strength, and strength is energy.

What did Abraham Lincoln say about that? The U.S. was in the midst of a horrendously divisive Civil War. "A house divided against itself cannot stand," he said. "I believe this government cannot endure, permanently half slave and half free."[8] Lincoln knew his scripture. He had seen the warning of Jesus in Matthew 12: "Every kingdom divided against itself is brought to desolation, and every city or house divided against itself will not stand."[9]

If we think of America's mission as a "Preamble of Freedom," it helps us to know how important it is to follow the path it sets forth. It is the leading light of our accountability to ourselves, as well as to our friends around the world. We can be free. So can the world. We can't make that happen for them. But we can set the example and do what we can to see that they can succeed on their own. Perhaps that won't happen on our time schedule, because it can only happen on theirs. Otherwise, remembering a childhood warning, we'll "cut off our nose to spite our face." Every action triggers a reaction. And over-reaction can lead to the under-performance of its intended effects. Remember Iraq.

That warning about over-reaction, for example, is why I never understood why "We the People" allowed the United States to rush into a war in Iraq that became so enormously expensive in lives lost, revenue squandered and credibility undermined. And I hope we never allow ourselves to do so again.

I will single out Dick Cheney, probably the most powerful vice president in the history of the United States, because I saw him in a different light than he is seen by many today. He was the House Minority Whip when I accompanied CSIS's CEO, Ambassador David Abshire,[10] on a visit to his spacious office on Capitol Hill. He was charming, smart, and cautious. I was the respectful note taker.

Cheney was an accomplished government servant over a long period of time. After Bill Clinton was elected President, he left Washington to take over the Halliburton Corporation in Texas, the supplier of billions of dollars worth of goods and services to the U.S. Military. In 2000, Presidential candidate George W. Bush asked him to suggest a running mate. He volunteered himself and, with W's election, there he was. Once in office, after 9-11 occurred, and the war machine cranked up, major contracts were signed with Halliburton.

Vice President Cheney was instrumental in persuading the nation and its leaders to go to war. In hindsight, this was a disastrous action that has had deep repercussions both for this nation and for the rest of the world today. As Fareed Zakaria recently reported, there is a straight line running from Iraq to the Islamic State. It wasn't Cheney's fault. We were all complicit.

In his farewell address of 1961, President Eisenhower famously warned against the unwarranted influence of what he called the "military industrial complex,"[11] which was an unofficial alliance of defense contractors and the armed forces, mediated by Congressmen who held the power of the purse. The iron triangle was hard at work in the aftermath of World War II.

"Ike" was a military leader who became an American hero. It goes without saying that he strongly supported our capacity to fight and win whatever battles were necessary to defeat the cold-blooded enemy. He was concerned that America not unwittingly undermine "the general Welfare" by overstocking our war machine. His remarks came after Korea and before Vietnam but while the draft was still in force. The Cold War was gearing up, and the first space shots were not yet in the air. There would be a great deal to take care of, and much for the nation and its leaders to handle, regarding the balance between peace and war.

In that same address, Ike was even more profound. He said: "Down the long lane of the history yet to be written America knows that this world of ours, ever growing smaller, must avoid becoming a community of dreadful fear and hate, and be instead a proud confederation of mutual trust and respect."

Continuing to speak about the world of nations, he went on to say this: "Such a confederation must be one of equals. The weakest must come to the same conference table as do we, protected as we are by our moral, economic, and military strength. That table, though scarred by many past frustrations, cannot be abandoned for the certain agony of the battlefield."

A mission of freedom has potential, but not automatic, energy. It is not so much a matter of force, because it takes the exercise of free will to accept it. It cannot be commanded, but it can be created and communicated. So, freedom comes down to being a gift which can be given and received by those who choose to be engaged. But they must choose to be engaged. So, the baton was passed and the "creative program" of engagement became that of President Kennedy and his successors.

Whoever the next President may be, that presumptive leader is accountable to the oath of office—to "preserve, protect and defend the Constitution of the United States"—taken before assuming the position. Those commitments and the responsibility to meet them, make that officeholder accountable to the highest law of public duty. The obligation is not to any other law or any other ideology. It has been and is agreed that no one is above the law of the land no matter what one's faith or other religious, spiritual, or economic pursuit may be.

The First Amendment protects all against any law of Congress that may abridge freedom of religion or limit speech, the press, assembly, or the expression of grievances. The Fourteenth Amendment grants each of us equal protection under the law. But neither authorizes anyone to use their freedom to violate another's freedom of choice. This is clearly the meaning of what the Constitution says.

Why then would we be so tied up in bureaucratic, legislative, and judicial knots? Action is extremely difficult to negotiate in the tangled government we have evolved over the years. Why? Because, as Philip Howard finds, we have taken cover in the literal language of the law rather than operating under its applicable meaning.[12] We have taken our constitutionally divided government and sub-divided its federal, state and local macrocosms of authority into microcosms of influence and resistance.

Excessively narrow interpretations of the law have stifled the spirit of the law. If we relied on officials to take full responsibility for how to apply the law, they would more likely be accountable for their actions. The essential meaning of the law is what counts – now. Any literal wording of the law cannot anticipate every circumstance.

The frustration and anger so often manifest by ordinary Americans today can be traced not only to the conduct of private citizens, but also to the conduct of public officials at local, state and national levels. The dysfunctional system is problem enough. As W. Edwards Deming has said: "a bad system will beat a good person every time." But the responses of the people make it better or worse. Systems can be turned around when leadership reassesses the mission and makes whatever judgments it takes to make it work. Not easy, not normal, but necessary.

Law enforcement officers cannot supplant irresponsible public officials any more than military officers can supplant civilian leaders, at least not in the American democracy. We are considering leadership, not management. The difference is the collaboration and consent that distinguishes how leadership works as distinct from the command and control that characterizes how management works. The most effective leadership is applied through the self-organized responses of hands-on professionals who are accountable for getting everything done. No room for tin soldiers.

In person, Sally Ride[13] did not come across as a leader. But she was. No flash or glamor there. She wasn't an imposing figure. She was small. Not a fancy talker. In fact, she was an optical physicist and the youngest astronaut—the first American woman and the only known LGBT person in space. And, she was a perfect example of a high-level hands-on professional. That's the way she came across in her visit at CSIS.

She was the only one to serve on both the investigating committees of the Challenger Disaster and the Columbia Disaster. She wrote and published children's books about science, and she worked on international security issues after retiring from NASA. Hands-on professionals have the advantage of knowledge-ability—they can walk the talk. She did that.

The meaning of the word preamble is derived—thank you to my no-nonsense high school Latin teachers Miss Darwin and Miss Winter[14]—from the Latin word "pre-ambulate," to walk before. To lead.

The Preamble leads the Constitution which is written in the name of "We the People." They are the ultimate leaders. But, government officials lead them. Leaders persuade. They teach. Leaders live by how well they help others whose best interests they serve, and not by whose personal preferences they may think they represent. These are not the same, or the sane, thing. To represent is to be a public servant, not merely a personal steward.

Stewardship is a trust. Trust is ownership. To be trustworthy is to own up to responsibility for taking care. Is not trust-building impartiality part of job one for any public servant? As Peter Drucker found in his decades with top level organizational executives, "Government degenerates into mediocrity and malperformance if it is not clearly accountable to someone for results." He continued: "Managing a business exclusively for the shareholders alienates the very people on whose motivation and dedication modern business depends, the knowledge workers." In learning organizations everyone is treated as a knowledge worker. There are no profits in the traditional sense. There are good returns on investment or poor ones. Do we know which are which?

"Unless we can learn how to increase the productivity of knowledge workers and service workers and increase it fast, the developed countries will face economic stagnation and severe social tension," Drucker concluded. "In knowledge and service work, partnership with the responsible worker is the only way to improve productivity. Nothing else works at all."[15]

Dan W. Dodson[16] was the son of a Texas sharecropper, and also a distinguished professor of sociology at New York University. He would enthrall his students with stories of helping Branch Rickey, President of the Brooklyn Dodgers, plan the acquisition and introduction of Jackie Robinson[17] as the first black player in Major League Baseball.

I was one of Dodson's students. I had to grudgingly admire Robinson's theatrical capabilities against my beloved Yankees, and had even bumped into him once at the front door of a Chock-Full-Of-Nuts Coffee Shop in midtown Manhattan. What made Dodson's stories so memorable, though, was how well they dramatized his theme of power and conflict in organizations. Robinson was a great American. Dodson helped explain why.

Professor Dodson came from an unlikely place to study, write and teach about the issue of legitimacy in the conduct of human communities. Legitimacy was a new concept for me. It refers to authenticity and the credibility that comes from having it. If one has it, then one can be trusted. Without that, leadership is hardly followed and barely present. Jackie Robinson had it because he earned it by displaying it. Authenticity is a precious possession too often absent in public officials as we watch them pay attention to trading favors.

XVI. AMERICAN SPIRIT

Is freedom a dynamic of the spirit? Yes. The energy of our spirit is our strength. This is where our freedom begins.

Without the focus of a transcending faith that centers the human spirit—however that faith may be expressed—people are more susceptible to compulsions of the moment. Those compulsions tear at the soul, and undermine the spirit and strength that come with it. As theologian Paul Tillich taught: "faith is a matter of freedom. Freedom is nothing more than the possibility of centered personal acts. In this respect, freedom and faith are identical."[1]

David Bohm[2] was a precocious young American from Wilkes Barre, Pennsylvania when he was run out of the country, like Sam Wanamaker, by Senator Joe McCarthy along with the House Un-American Activities Committee. Bohm ended up in England where he became the discoverer, as both a physicist and philosopher, of what his biographer called "infinite potential." He and Einstein were both physicists and philosophers as well as friends and collaborators who happened to cross the Atlantic in different directions with cosmic maps in their minds, imagining the world as it is and as it would be.

Infinite potential, Bohm explained, is the "energy of spirit"[3] that is manifest in the human spirit, which is the oxygen of body and soul. This energy of spirit literally comes to us from the infinite from which all that is finite or physical is created, as Bohm pointed out. As such, this energy of spirit is never born and never dies. It is simply there for us to celebrate and use. Like water—drink it and be well. Why do we remember the words Buzz Lightyear proclaimed in the *Toy Story* movie: "To infinity and beyond"?[4] Do his words beckon us? Is that why we feel called by them?

Einstein was not an atheist. He was born a Jew in Germany and accepted God as "the Old One." He said "the Lord is subtle, but he is not malicious." He observed that "every one who is seriously involved in the pursuit of science becomes convinced that a spirit is manifest in the laws of the Universe—a spirit vastly superior to that of man, and one in the face of which we with our modest powers must feel humble." He thought that "science without religion is lame," and he also thought that "religion without science is blind." He believed that:

> *"Science can only ascertain what is, but not what should be, and outside of its domain value judgments of all kinds remain necessary. Religion, on the other hand, deals only with evaluations of human thought and action; it does not analyze scientifically verifiable facts and relationships between facts."*[5]

What did Einstein mean when he mentioned "a spirit vastly superior to that of man—in the face of which we with our modest powers must feel humble?" Lorenz's "butterfly effect" came after Einstein's death, and I wonder about its relationship to his idea. After all, when we humans "flap our wings" in a given situation at any moment in time, we might be more sensitive to our collective dependence on the initial conditions in which we flapped our wings. Because our conduct has its consequences.

Our creative energy may be drawn into a center of gravity with that of other butterflies which mushrooms into a critical mass and explodes with a chain reaction felt far beyond the place where it began. Isn't this, in effect, what happens when sudden disturbances burst into our public lives? Why would the laws of nature apply in one circumstance but not another?

We may not have all the facts. We may not have formed all our opinions. And we certainly do not know all the leaders of the people. But what we can do is what we all already do, every day. We can turn on the blind vision that Frederick Jervis called for; we can ask ourselves what we think; and then we can start planning and managing our plans in every way we can. We will then be leading our lives in ways most likely to help the country because we will be discovering always more deeply and richly who we are and what we hope for. And we will be doing that as one people, with liberty and justice for all.

Bob Galvin[6] was chairman of Motorola, the multinational telecommunications company headquartered in Schaumburg, Illinois, where the Six Sigma quality improvement process, which became the gold standard in world manufacturing, was invented. It received the first Malcolm Baldridge National Quality Award given by the President of the United States for performance excellence in systems productivity. A year later, the Center for Strategic & International Studies invited Galvin to join its first Board of Trustees, and I had the pleasure of getting to know him.

What I remember best was his indomitable spirit. It was displayed in the photo he kept on his desk shaking hands in friendship with Sony CEO Akio Morita while both wore bathing suits.[7] That spirit was also displayed in his wearing a BOB Galvin name tag on his shirt—no suit jacket—and being greeted by custodians in the office elevator, and later, by his reciting Shakespeare on stage in Chicago at a benefit for the Globe Theatre about to be built in London. This was all highly unusual, but for him it was perfectly natural. People loved and respected him. All enjoyed themselves. Everyone seemed to be doing their best. The extraordinary performance of the company seemed to follow.

The human spirit is where we start with our freedom and our future. The Preamble of Freedom holds the infinite potential which belongs to us all. And remember what Yogi Berra said: "*It ain't over till it's over.*" That was after his team came from behind to win the pennant and the World Series. Don't forget what he also said: "*the future ain't what it used to be.*"[8] Yogi is remembered in the Hall of Fame, and was getting around in a wheelchair, enjoying the love of baseball fans everywhere when he recently passed away.

Robert Heilbroner, writing over half a century ago, was not an optimist. I based one of my history classes at UT on his book *The Future As History*,[9] which was about shaping the meander of events and the vacillating influences of leadership, from the bestial to the beautiful. "More than anything else," he said, "our disorientation before the future reveals a loss of our historic identity, an incapacity to grasp our historic situation." In our Constitution, of course, that takes us back to the Preamble.

Heilbroner held a dim view of current affairs, both in general and particular by those going on in America. Yet he observed that, "with all its glaring and inexcusable failures, the United States is still probably the most favored and favorable place on earth for a child to be born and to grow up." He called for "fortitude and understanding" as the two qualities most needed to preserve "the integrity of the very idea of progress itself."

"Particularly for Americans," he concluded, this will provide "a test of the spirit." No doubt Heilbroner would agree with Woody Allen's observation: "I'm not afraid to die. I just don't want to be there when it happens."[10] That's at least one way to focus more energy on avoiding catastrophe. Fear—it can work, but is it the recommended route?

When Francis Scott Key[11] wrote the words which became our national anthem following the British bombardment of Fort McHenry, that was America's last holdout in the War of 1812, he finished with those wonderful words: *"And the Star-Spangled Banner in triumph shall wave, O'er the land of the free and the home of the brave."* The Americans had driven the British fleet out to sea, and defended their freedom as a new nation.

On "The Day of Infamy,"[12] as President Roosevelt called it, December 7, 1941, the Japanese admiral who was the primary architect of the raid on Pearl Harbor that tragic day observed, "I fear all we have done is to awaken a sleeping giant and fill him with a terrible resolve."[13] There is no doubt that America had a fierce resolve, and it worked to our advantage then because the American people rallied behind the defense of freedom and world opinion supported it.

The same was true for just a short time after 9-11. Then, the American-led response divided public opinion at home and around the world, and the lack of a unified political will undercut the probabilities that a comprehensive strategy could overcome the support for terrorism that was behind the attacks. The American spirit was not in it. A confident morale never took hold. And a strong resolve did not materialize.

The "Blessings of Liberty," which are timelessly inscribed in the message of the Preamble, did not appear magically out of nowhere. They came from the courageous response of willful leaders who didn't give up until they had created an architecture of freedom. They made it the heart of the nation.

Courage leads to confidence. And we move ahead. We pre-ambulate—we walk before all else to come. We connect with our sisters and our brothers. A network forms and expands. It grows into a mass of humanity connected electronically, spiritually and in person, as far as the message can reach. That has happened before. Thank you Moses, Jesus, and Muhammad, and all the prophets everywhere.[14]

Their leadership came from a deeply embedded certainty of who they were and what they were meant to do. Their freedom of conscience—their faith, their thoughts, and their expression— produced a spiritual energy of such superior force that it continues to reach far beyond the momentary physical presence of their time, to this day and for the ages to come.

Today, America isn't engaged in a declared war, but we have been engaged in the moral equivalent of war for which our readiness is in question. This different kind of war is more than a walk for freedom embraced by people of good will. It is a moral march against barbarity that challenges civilization. Our American crisis of freedom is part of a global crisis, a meta crisis in which multiple threats confront the civilized world and challenge its ability to respond prudently and wisely for a future of prosperity for all.

It is time for a reality check. The Preamble of the U.S. Constitution is the gravitational center from which to lead the effort because it contains the possibility of a "new leadership ethic." New, that is, to the practice of responsibility which has long been seen as something to be managed, not led. Such an ethic has four insufficiently recognized dimensions: doing the greatest good; for the largest number of people; over the longest period of time; at the lowest cost of resources.

This, I submit, is a statement of moral principle that may be converted to and combined with practical considerations. It works prospectively, as does the great equivalency translator, in which the greatest good is our creative energy, the largest number of people is our critical mass, and the longest period of time at the lowest cost of resources is our chain reaction. Thus, we pre-ambulate to the future—yes, this is the way we can lead.

The greatest good embraces the wider community and considers what's best for it as a whole. *The largest number* envisages reaching to everyone as an individual person. *The longest period* looks forward as far as the mind can see or imagine. *The lowest cost* requires the most effective, economical, and therefore, most efficient use of all human and material resources.

The new leadership ethic is the embodiment of the Preamble as it is put into practice. All four dimensions of the ethic—the good, the people, the time, and the cost—are addressed in the ten cardinal principles of the Preamble: People, Union, Justice, Tranquility, defence, Welfare, Liberty, Posterity, Constitution, America.

During the Pope's visit to America, he concluded his message to Congress by saying:

> *"In these remarks I have sought to present some of the richness of your cultural heritage, of the spirit of the American people. It is my desire that this spirit continue to develop and grow, so that as many young people as possible can inherit and dwell in a land which has inspired so many people to dream. God bless America!"*[15]

Our meta crisis must be met with our meta force. That is freedom and that is our challenge—to use or to lose. Hold on to our values. Release our energies. Bless the world with our gift of freedom. The

Preamble is America's soul and its DNA. Let us pre-ambulate into our future together with our soul, by our solidarity, to our mutual security.

XVII. CLOSING DEAL

Does America have what it takes? Yes. The genesis of our law is an exodus to an order that creates a revelation of freedom.

Embedded in the first sentence of the U.S. Constitution—the oldest written constitution in the world—are America's greatest energies as a nation—straight from its heart. When we read The Preamble closely, we will discover that the energy it embodies, in one form or another, is the creative energy that can lead to the realization of our nation state and its influence on the rest of the world as we know it. Creative energy is what matters most because it leads to a critical mass of public opinion moving at the light speed of an electronic universe, attracting and affecting everything else— our society, our world and our spirits.

The Preamble presents the standards by which we can be called to account as a nation. Our method of doing that must meet the highest standard available. That would be the law of universal creativity embedded in the algorithm of universal energy. This law and its algorithm are embodied in the familiar formulation known as $E=mc^2$ which symbolizes the transformation of electrical energy that pulses throughout the universe. This energy is the power source of all creativity as it transforms into critical mass through sustainable chain reactions of strength. Its results produce the world as a system and "We the People" as interdependent parts of it.

Proposition one: So, we are on solid ground to consider the first point of the Preamble's accountability from this source of potential energy, namely its **founding purpose.** The **E** of this algorithm represents the potential of all creative **energy.** This potential is the purpose of the Preamble and the **Drive** of America's **DNA**: "We the People of the United States, in Order to form a more perfect Union..." The idea the founders had in mind was to transform a confederation of divided states into a federation of united states in accordance with the political authority and civic virtue of the people. This drive is the soul and the creative seed of our nation. The first

155

issue, then, will be to separate this **common problem** of purpose from all the rest.

Proposition two: Based on this grounding, we may continue to consider the Preamble's accountability on the points of its **operating principles**, which are the means by which the purpose reaches its goal. These principles, taken together, are the kinetic energy, or energy-in-motion, that creates the property of **mass—m**—in our energy algorithm. This mass determines the strength of our mutual gravitational attraction to other bodies and defines the content of the system. These principles are to—"establish Justice, insure domestic Tranquility, provide for the common defence, promote the general Welfare." They enable the formation of a center of gravity which may grow to a tipping point of critical mass. Collectively they are the **Nucleus** of the **DNA**. This nucleus is America's solidarity, its national unity. The second issue, then, is how this identification of core **civic interests** can be separated from the diversity of partisan political interests.

Proposition three: What consummates the Preamble's accountability is its promise of sustainability. That is its **final result,** the ability to realize the action words "and secure the Blessings of Liberty to ourselves and our Posterity." This point draws on the pull of electromagnetic power from the constancy of **light**, or c^2 in our algorithm. This induces a chain reaction of continuous impact. And this is where the **Acceleration** of **DNA** assures its durability. This acceleration is our national security in the form of America's partnerships both in the homeland and internationally. This is the third issue, where **mutual gains** with each of our partners bring us to the common ground of shared service and protection.

Proposition four: The fourth and final issue concerns **objective criteria**—what it means when we "do ordain and establish this Constitution for the United States of America" as the Preamble concludes. Does the **DNA** of the Preamble lead the way to a "land of the free and home of the brave"? Measured against that standard and criteria: is this true enough today? When we consider, indeed calculate, the productivity of all the principles together—from the purpose, through its operations, to its results as a single electromagnetic force field—have we achieved the promise of America's **DNA** through its Preamble? In the real world, an electromagnetic field is drawn to a gravitational force, and the gravitational force with the greatest mass has the strongest attraction. Have we got our freedom meta force going?

There are **four reasons** why we can honor the Preamble now by pledging to make it our guide star and tool of measurement.

The Constitution is, with a first sentence of law as its Preamble, a **benevolent doctrine** for the people of this nation that was founded as a light for the old world. By following its spirit, its guidance, and its principles "We the People" are given a positive, problem-solving, workable way in which to approach public issues. Because it begins with "We the People of the United States, in Order to form a more perfect Union," we, as the people, are seen to be the ultimate civil authority. The responsibility, then, from the moment we accept it, is ours. There is, then, no remote civil authority above or beyond. Rather, our collective authority is here and now. The people and their uniting to form a more perfect union, is our purpose. Government shutdowns be damned! Aren't they contrary to the Preamble of the Constitution and, therefore, to the Constitution itself?

Our world of **high technology** is enabling us to connect with others nearly everywhere and almost instantly. Telecommunications have become interpersonal, international and disruptive – simultaneously. The micro and the macro are at once cosmic. The microscope, the telescope, and the stethoscope allow us to look at things in all ways all the time. To "establish Justice, insure domestic Tranquility, provide for the common defence, [and] promote the general Welfare" are useful operating principles to help us sort out our real interests and then address our responsibilities to foster their realization. They also serve as standards for measuring our progress.

The world of **global knowledge** that is a-dawning today is impressive and potentially overwhelming. It comes at us from all directions. We are faced with information on the fly, data at every doorway, knowledge in pieces and parcels. Hopefully amongst all

157

this there is a semblance of wisdom. How do we sort it all out? Where is the meaning in it all? What are the core values we share to help us, as a nation, find the answers?

Can "We the People" "secure the Blessings of Liberty to ourselves and our Posterity" as we do that? We need to realize that we have these values in our hands: people and union are the founding principles of purpose; justice, tranquility, defense and welfare are our operating principles in practice; while liberty and posterity are the principles by which we judge our final results in the name of our Constitution and our Nation. Our mutual gains arise from the interaction of these values at any given time.

To positively and successfully undertake a role of **mass leadership** in this world we are now part of, we have a benevolent doctrine, high technology and global knowledge. What is needed then is a set of objective criteria against which to measure our progress. The principles set forth in the Preamble are those criteria. So, when the Preamble concludes that its words "do ordain and establish this Constitution for the United States of America," it is simply saying that it is the lead-in of the Law of the Land.

I set forth here **ten questions** that flow from the Preamble now before us as a nation as we consider our response to the challenges we have as a republic, as Ben Franklin said, "if you can keep it:"

Question #1: How can "We the People of the United States" reclaim the human heart of the American political system in place of the limitless influence of money that now dominates political campaigns?

Question #2: How do we enable voting by everyone eligible to vote in every election for public office in the country "in Order to form a more perfect Union?"

Question #3: How do we "establish Justice » under law through equal opportunity, equal protection and equal treatment of every person always?

158

Question #4: How do we "insure domestic Tranquility" so that the private lives of people are not disturbed by the destructive behavior of anyone or anything?

Question #5: How do we obtain the full participation of every American citizen and every nation of the world to "provide for the common defence?"

Question #6: How do we "promote the general Welfare" of those who are able, and assistance for those who are not, so everyone can be productive in some way and share in the fruits of this production?

Question #7: How can we "secure the Blessings of Liberty" through the promotion and practice of civic virtue by helping to generate the greatest knowledge-ability that can be acquired by each and every one?

Question #8: How can we most responsibly sustain this liberty "to ourselves and our Posterity" in order to secure it for the generations to come both here and everywhere?

Question #9: How can we pay our highest respect and give our greatest assurance to the fact that the Constitution, as the Law of the Land from first sentence to last, is the foundation and the DNA of "We the People" who did "ordain and establish this Constitution?"

Question #10: How can we, no longer citizens of separate states under the original Articles of Confederation, live, work, and support each other as citizens "for the United States of America" under the Constitution?

These are the ten questions I would like to see every candidate for public office answer—each in the domains of their own service—as part of their political campaigns. And then I would hope that they would pledge to follow the promises made and report to "We the People" how they have fulfilled their pledge.

Finally, it is time to challenge America's best entrepreneurial and creative minds and entrepreneurial talents, however organized, to imagine and create a *Pre-Ambulating Model of America's Promise* (PAMAP) to analyze and evaluate its condition on an annual basis. The idea of an American Promise model is to give everyone ready access to the general condition of the country based on its freedom of creativity which is the root of our productivity. This would help us keep tabs on how we're currently doing with our Declaration of Independence that, in 1776, said:

> **"We hold these truths to be self-evident that all men are created equal, that they are endowed by their Creator with certain unalienable Rights, that among these are Life, Liberty and the pursuit of Happiness."**

Even Vladimir Putin cited America's creativity when asked what he most admired about America. "Creativity when it comes to your tackling problems. Their openness: openness and open-mindedness —because it allows them to unleash the inner potential of their people. And thanks to that, America has attained such amazing results in developing their country."[1]

In PAMAP, each of the Preamble's ten points—People, Union, Justice, Tranquility, defence, Welfare, Liberty, Posterity, Constitution, America—would serve as a constitutional standard of measurement against which national performance qualities would be compared.

These are the sacred principles on which our country has been built and is to be governed. When claims are made about taking a principled view of the Constitution, these are the principles about which we are talking.

Each of these ten standards would be divided into performance indicators that would categorize significant specialized activities. Each of the indicators would be networked with each of the others to produce a more comprehensive analysis of American realities at any given point in time—say, annually. By themselves, they would be instructive. Networked together, they would be illuminating. We would be able to see and describe situations more clearly than ever before. Inter-relationships not previously understood would be more obviously in evidence.

These analyses would, then, be the foundation of evaluations that are enumerated to produce a set of metrics. Each metric would be the descriptor of a qualitative nature, like taking one's temperature or checking one's blood pressure. There are many examples from the business world that can serve as guideposts for the formulation of these metrics.[2] There are also a number of quality of life tools to assess perceptions and status.[3] The PAMAP metrics would be windows into the wilderness of undeciphered realities whose characteristics ought to be known.

All of these metrics would be calculated by a set of algorithms that stem from Einstein's universal accounting tool, which shows, as Brian Greene has reminded us, that "there is nothing you can do that doesn't tap directly into $E=mc^2$." In computer lingo, this is the creative program, for better or worse, which triggers the way things happen. By virtue of Einstein's equivalence of mass and energy, the more energy poured into a situation, the more mass comes out of it. And by the logic of computer microscopy, the more energy there is to spend, the more specific details one can see. Everything we know, from spirits to specifics, works according to that formulation.

These metrics would headline an annual PAMAP report for discussion by the public, the press, and officials. These discussions, then, would lead the way to any modifications of law and regulations that would address the findings—to keep us free—right from our heart.

CHAPTER NOTES
INTRODUCTION

1. http://pandce.proboards.com/thread/498038/life-time-mass-shootings. This sentiment was earlier advanced by the U.S. Attorney General http://abcnews.go.com/US/attorney-general-sad-fact-safe-now/story?id=33481933.

2. Carson, Ben (with Candy Carson). (2015) *A More Perfect Union*. Sentinel, An imprint of Penguin Random House. New York.

I. FIRST FACT

1. Hoffer, Peter Charles: (2013) *For Ourselves and Our Posterity: The Preamble to the Federal Constitution in American History*. Oxford University Press, New York.

2. http://press-pubs.uchicago.edu/founders/documents/a2_2-3s15.html

3. Federalist Papers #78.

4. Suri, Jeremi, (2011) *Liberty's Surest Guardian: American Nation-Building from the Founders to Obama*. Free Press. New York.

5. Pope Francis address to U.S. Congress: Holy See Press Office. Sept. 20,2015.www.usccb.org/about/leadership/holy-see/francis/papal-visit-2015.

6. Hoffer, *Op. cit.*

7. Hoffer, *Op. cit.*

II. FREE COUNTRY

http://www.historycommons.org/context.jsp?item=a090874twaflight841

See Chapter X. Mike Finegan information at http://gsnmagazine.com/article/42480/fbispecialagentmikefinnegan%E2%80%99srelentlesspursu

Eisenhower "Farewell Address"- TV Broadcast: www.youtube.com/watch?v=CWiYW_FBfY

Fineman, Howard. (2009). *The Thirteen American Arguments: Enduring Debates That Define and Inspire Our Country.* Random House, New York.

http://constitutioncenter.org/learn/educational-resources/historical-documents/perspectives-on-the-constitution-a-republic-if-you-can-keep-it

Pope Francis. *Op. cit.*

https://books.google.com/books?id=t6Ynu-b9vrUC&pg=PT18&lpg=PT18&dq=sought+the+stability+and+strength+that+could+come+from+union+and+from+steady,+effective+government&source=bl&ots=Zt0yIBMcv2&sig=zykTQho8YsPnU7mOUIDfzr59BXo&hl=en&sa=X&ved=0ahUKEwjOkqTvgsrJAhUBGj4KHevYBA0Q6AEIHjAA#v=onepage&q=sought%20the%20stability%20and%20strength%20that%20could%20come%20from%20union%20and%20from%20steady%2C%20effective%20government&f=false1

https://books.google.com/books?id=t6Ynu-b9vrUC&pg=PT18&lpg=PT18&dq=sought+the+stability+and+strength+that+could+come+from+union+and+from+steady,+effective+government&source=bl&ots=Zt0yIBMcv2&sig=zykTQho8YsPnU7mOUIDfzr59BXo&hl=en&sa=X&ved=0ahUKEwjOkqTvgsrJAhUBGj4KHevYBA0Q6AEIHjAA#v=onepage&q=sought%20the%20stability%20and%20strength%20that%20could%20come%20from%20union%20and%20from%20steady%2C%20effective%20government&f=false

http://avalon.law.yale.edu/18th_century/artconf.asp

http://www.motherjones.com/politics/2015/06/neil-young-donald-trump-bernie-sanders

http://teachingamericanhistory.org/library/document/an-act-for-freedom-of-onscience/

For Yogi's top quotes see: www.retroglaxy.com/sports/yogi-berra.asp.

See Commanger. *Op cit.* Gettysburg Address

Grisworld, Wendy. (2013) *Cultures and Societies in a Changing World.* Sage, Los Angeles, CA

III. LEADING EDGE

1. Roger Williams, Founder of Rhode Island, Arrived in Boston February 5, 1631. Williams founded the colony of RhodeIsland based upon principles of complete religious toleration, separation of church and state, and political democracy (values that the U.S. would later be founded upon). It became a refuge for people persecuted for their religious beliefs. After forming the first Baptist church in America, Williams left it to seek spirituality in different ways. He stopped preaching to his friends, the Indians, when he realized that their form of worship also fell under his principle of religious freedom. He declared, "forced worship stinks in God's nostrils." Williams' ideas were radical at the time, but can you imagine living in a place without religious freedom now? http://www.americaslibrary.gov/jb/colonial/jb_colonial_williams_4.html

2. Born on August 1, 1779, in Frederick County, Maryland, Francis Scott Key became a lawyer who witnessed the British attack on Fort McHenry during the War of 1812. The fort withstood the day-long assault, inspiring Key to write a poem that would become the future U.S. national anthem, "The Star-Spangled Banner." Key later served as a district attorney for Washington, D.C. He died on January 11, 1843.http://www.biography.com/people/francis-scott-key-9364165#synopsis

3. Wood, Gordon S., (2012) *The Idea of America: Reflections on the Birth of the United States.* Penguin Press, New York.

4. Juergensmeyer, Mark. (3rd ed. 2003). University of California Press. London, England

5. "Duty, honor, country. These three hallowed words reverently dictate what you ought to be, what you can be, what you will be.

They are your rallying point to build courage when courage seems to fail, to regain faith when there seems to be little cause for faith, to create hope when hope becomes forlorn." General of the Army Douglas MacArthur to the cadets at the U.S. Military Academy in accepting the Sylvanus Thayer Award on May 12, 1962. www.jsums.edu/arotc/duty-honor-country.

6. Peters, Thomas J. and Waterman Jr., Robert H. *In Search of Excellence: Lessons from America.* (2004) Harper Collins. New York.

7. Peters. *Op. cit.*

8. www.biography.com/people/adolf-hitler-9340144

9. Former Ambassador to NATO, Abshire, David. *Preventing World War III: A Realistic Grand Strategy.* (1989) Harper Collins, New York.

10. Tech experts call this kind of thing 'siloing.' Per businessdictionary.com, an information silo is "an information management system that is unable to communicate with other information management systems." While we're depending on this system for informative material, it's tailoring its answers to what it thinks we want to know or it wants us to know. Hate groups or political factions like ISIS that draw strength by word-of-mouth can grow with the help of the Internet. The belief that climate change isn't real, that sustainable farming can't succeed globally or that the middle ground can't be reached between two sides seems more at the heart of what we stand to lose from automated siloing of our news.

11. Drucker, Peter. (2011) *Post-Capitalist Society.* Butterworth-Heinemann. Abingdon, Oxon, England and New York.

12. For a list of mass murder shooters see: http://www.cnn.com/2013/09/16/us/20-deadliest-mass-shootings-in-u-s-history-fast-facts/

13. Take, for instance, the rise of and use of "Joe the Plumber" in the 2008 Presidential campaign. According to David Macaray:. "Anyone who followed the 2008 presidential campaign is bound to recall Samuel Joseph Wurzelbacher, the man who was plucked out of obscurity by Republican candidate John McCain to be paraded around as "Joe the Plumber," intended, presumably, to represent the voice of the American Everyman. What made Joe so damned

infuriating was his annoying combination of abysmal ignorance and near suffocating arrogance. While practically every word out of his mouth was factually inaccurate or unsupportable, he uttered them with the supreme confidence of a Nobel Laureate." http://www.huffingtonpost.com/david-macaray/remembering-joe-the-plumb_b_7843822.html

14. De Tocqueville, Alexis. (2003) *Democracy in America and Two Essays.* Penguin Books, London, England and New York.

15. John 8:32 New Revised Standard: "Then you will know the truth, and the truth will set you free." For a good discuss-ion on this subject, see: https://www.psychologytoday.com/blog/the-second-noble-truth/201205/the-truth-will-not-set-you-free.

IV. INVOLUNTARY SERVITUDE

1. Mental Health America.www.mentalhealthamerica.net/co dependency.

2. www.cbsnews,com/news/hidden-holocaust-60minutes

3. Articles.chicagotribune.com/keyword/frank-borman

4. Devlin, Patrick. (1965) *The Enforcement of Morals.* London.

5. Torrey E. Fuller. M.D. *Frontier Justice: The Rise and Fall of the Loomis Gang*

6. Ghandi, Mahatma. (1965) *Ghandi on Non-Violence.* New Directions Publishing, New York.

7. http://www.asa3.org/ASA/education/views/invariance.htm

8. http://library.timelesstruths.org/music/Rock_of_Ages/+852

9. Cheshire, Richard D. (2003).*Leading by Heart: Through the World of Quantum Physics.* Fithian Press, Santa Barbara. CA.

10. Fineman, Howard. Op. cit.

11. http://www.hartsookcompanies.com/press_release/press_frantzreb.shtml

12. http://www.newyorker.com/magazine/2014/09/pictures-institution

13. *Colgate-Palmolive Company History: Creating Bright Smiles*
    www.colgate.com/app/Colgate/US/Corp/.../1806.cvsp

V. SYSTEM CONFIDENCE

1. George Soros' Open Society:
   https://www.opensocietyfoundations.org/about

2. http://www.holisticwisdom.org/hwpages/chapt%202%20-%20GST.htm

3. http://fractalfoundation.org/resources/what-is-chaos-theory/

4. https://www.washingtonpost.com/world/in-tunisia-act-of-one-fruit-vendor-sparks-wave-of-revolution-through-arabworld/2011/03/16/AFjfsueB_story.html

5. Peter Senge is a leading writer in the area of learning organizations. His seminal works, *The Fifth Discipline: The Art and Practice of the Learning Organization*, and *The Fifth Discipline Fieldbook: Strategies and Tools for Building a Learning Organization*, describe five disciplines that must be mastered when introducing learning into an organization. To summarize, a learning organization does away with the mindset that it is only senior management who can and do all the thinking for an entire corporation. Learning organizations challenge all employees to tap into their inner resources and potential, in hopes that they can build their own community based on principles of liberty, humanity, and a collective will to learn. See: http://www.moyak.com/papers/learning-organization.html

6. Cheshire. *Op. cit.*

7. https://www.ut.edu/Content.aspx?id=15884

8. ttp://www.tbo.com/south-tampa/perry-harvey-jr-tampas-first-black-councilman-dies-at—498535

9. http://www.zoominfo.com/p/Moses-Sawney/589744363

10. Senge, Peter M. (2006), *The Fifth Discipline: The Art & Practice of The Learning Organization.* Doubleday, New York.

11. Babbie, Earl. (2013). *The Practice of Social Research.* Cengage Learning, Boston, MA.

VI. BIG PICTURE

1. There have been several thoughtful discussions about a 'grand strategy' recently. See the testimony before the Senate Armed Serivcesl Committee by General Jim Mathis of the Hoover Institute on January 27, 2015. http://www.hoover.org/research/new-american-grand-strategy

2. See, for instance, the 3D Planning Guide: Diplomacy, Develop-ment, Defense 31 July, 2012. https://www.usaid.gov/sites/default/files/documents/1866/3D%20Plan ning%20Guide_Update_FINAL%20(31%20Jul%2012).pdf

3. Natural law definition: The doctrine that human affairs should be governed by ethical principal that are part of the very nature of things and that can be understood by reason. The first paragraphs of the Declaration of Independence contain a clear statement of the doctrine.

4. 9-11 Final Report: http://www.911commission.gov/report/911Report_Exec.pdf

5. Gödel's theorem says in understandable terms that there are ALWAYS more things that are true than you can prove. Any system of logic or numbers that mathematicians ever came up with will always rest on at least a few unprovable assumptions. Gödel's Incompleteness Theorem applies not just to math, but to *everything* that is subject to the laws of logic. Incompleteness is true in math; it's equally true in science or language or philosophy. And: If the universe is mathematical and logical, Incompleteness also applies to the universe. See *Godel's Proof* by Ernest Nagel and James R. Newman, published in 1958 and released in paperback by New York University Press in 1983.

6. Heisenberg's uncertainty principle: The more precisely the position is determined, the less precisely the momentum is known in this instant, and vice versa. Heisenberg, uncertainty paper, 1927. For more explanation see: https://www.aip.org/history/heisenberg/p08.htm

7. For information on Isaac Asimov and his 500 books, etc. See his homepage.' You will find there pretty much all you may want to know–and more. http://www.asimovonline.com/asimov_home_page.html

8. David Shipler: Career & Experience:

168

Joined The New York Times as a news clerk in 1966 & two years later he was promoted to city staff reporter, in which he covered housing, poverty and politics.-Served as a New York Times correspondent in Saigon, covering South Vietnam, Cambodia, Laos, Thailand, as well as Burma. -Correspondent in Moscow Bureau for four years (1975-79); - Moscow Bureau Chief from 1977-79 Served as Bureau Chief of The New York Times in Jerusalem.

9. See: http://www.csmonitor.com/Commentary/Opinion/2010/0126/Is-America-still-the-last-best-hope-of-earth) which still seems quite appropriate: "In his annual message to Congress in 1862, Lincoln argued that emancipation was actually the straightest path to victory, because only by giving "freedom to the slave" would Americans "assure freedom to the free." By making freedom the war's issue, Americans would keep alive a flame that only they, among all the nations of the earth, were tending. On the other hand, if Americans had lost heart for freedom, then the whole experiment in democratic government which began in 1776 might as well be called off for good. Abolishing the last vestige of un-freedom in America would become the measure of whether we would 'nobly save, or meanly lose, the last best hope of earth."

10. Senge. *Op. cit.*

11. Fisher, Roger; Ury, William; Patton, Bruce. (2011) *Getting to Yes; Negotiating Agreement Without Giving In.* Penguin, New York.

VII. BLIND VISION

1. Ainsworth-Land, George T. & Jarman, Beth. (1992). *Breakpoint and Beyond: Making the Future – Today.* Harper Business, New York.

2. http://www.legacy.com/obituaries/unionleader/obituary.aspx?pid=17226010

3. http://www.goodreads.com/quotes/44564-for-the-simplicity-on-this-side-of-complexity-i-wouldnt

4. Gordon Wood, *The American Idea. Op cit.*

5. Siegel, Bernie. (2011) *Love, Medicine & Miracles: Lessons Learned About Self-Healing from a Surgeon's Experience with Exceptional Patients.* Harper Collins, New York.

6. Rebecca Chopp- http://news.colgate.edu/2009/05/rebecca-chopp-reflects-on-tenu.html/

7. Henry George "Hank" Steinbrenner III is part-owner and co-chairman of the New York Yankees. He is the older brother of principal owner and managing general partner Hal Steinbrenner. https://en.wikipedia.org/wiki/Hank_Steinbrenner

8. George Steinbrenner, who bought a declining Yankees team in 1973, promised to stay out of its daily affairs and then, in an often tumultuous reign, placed his formidable stamp on 7 World Series championship teams, 11 pennant winners and a sporting world powerhouse valued at perhaps $1.6 billion, lived in Tampa, Fla. Mr. Steinbrenner — who came to be known as the Boss — and the Yankees thrived through all the arguments, all the turmoil, all the bombast. http://www.nytimes.com/2010/07/14/sports/baseball/14steinbrenner.html

9. http://www.clubofrome.org/index.php/mankind-at-the-turning-point-1974/

10. Pope's address to Congress, *Op. cit.*

11. http://www.usa-flag-site.org/song-lyrics/america/

VIII. FREEDOM GATES

1. Magna Carta, meaning 'The Great Charter', is one of the most famous documents in the world. Originally issued by King John of Eng-land (1199-1216) as a practical solution to the political crisis he faced in 1215, Magna Carta established for the first time the principle that every-body, including the king, was subject to the law. Buried within the 63 clauses were a number of fundamental values that both challenged the autocracy of the king and proved highly adaptable in future centuries. Most famously, the 39th clause gave all 'free men' the right to justice and a fair trial. Some of Magna Carta's core principles are echoed in the United States Bill of Rights (1791) and in many other constitutional documents around the world, as well as in the Universal Declaration of Human Rights (1948) and the European Convention on Human Rights (1950). - See more at:http://www.bl.uk/magna-carta/articles/magna-carta-anintroduction#sthash.cpmggoxG.dpuf

2. The Enlightenment or 'Age of Reason' was a period in the late seventeenth century and early eighteenth century, where a group of philosophers, scientists and thinkers advocated new ideas based on reason. This period saw a decline in the power of absolute monarchies, a decline in the pre-eminence of the church and a rise of modern political ideologies, such as liberalism, republicanism and greater independence of thought.
   See:http://www.history.com/topics/enlightenment

3. http://teachingamericanhistory.org/library/document/an-act-for-freedom-of-conscience/

4. Gordon Wood. *Op. cit.*

5. The first 10 amendments to the Constitution make up the Bill of Rights. Written by James Madison in response to calls from several states for greater constitutional protection for individual liberties, the Bill of Rights lists specific prohibitions on governmental power. The Virginia Declaration of Rights, written by George Mason, strongly influenced Madison. One of the many points of contention between Federalists and Anti-Federalists was the Constitution's lack of a bill of rights that would place specific limits on government power. Madison went through the Constitution itself, making changes where he thought most appropriate. But several Representatives, led by Roger Sherman, objected that Congress had no authority to change the wording of the Constitution itself. Therefore, Madison's changes were presented as a list of amendments that would follow Article VII.
   http://www.billofrightsinstitute.org/founding-ocuments/bill-of-rights/

6. "That on the first day of January, in the year of our Lord one thousand eight hundred and sixty-three, all persons held as slaves within any State or designated part of a State, the people whereof shall then be in rebellion against the United States, shall be then, thenceforward, and forever free; and the Executive Government of the United States, including the military and naval authority thereof, will recognize and maintain the freedom of such persons, and will do no act or acts to repress such persons, or any of them, in any efforts they may make for their actual freedom." See:
   www.archives.gov/exhibits/featureddocuments/emancipationproclamation/transcript.html for full text.

7. Amendment XIII: Section 1. Neither slavery nor involuntary servitude, except as a punishment for crime whereof the party shall have been duly convicted, shall exist within the United States, or any place subject to their jurisdiction.

8. www.law.cornell.edu/constitution/amendmenttxiv.

   The Fourteenth Amendment addresses many aspects of citizenship and the rights of citizens. The most commonly used and frequently litigated -phrase in the amendment is "equal protection of the laws", which figures prominently in a wide variety of landmark cases, including Brown v. Board of Education (racial discrimination), Roe v. Wade (reproductive rights), Bush v. Gore (election recounts), Reed v. Reed (gender discrimination), and University of California v. Bakke (racial quotas in education). *Amendment XIV:* Section 1. All persons born or naturalized in the United States, and subject to the jurisdiction thereof, are citizens of the United States and of the state wherein they reside. No state shall make or enforce any law which shall abridge the privileges or immunities of citizens of the United States; nor shall any state deprive any person of life, liberty, or property, without due process of law; nor deny to any person within its jurisdiction the equal protection of the laws.

9. Amendment XIX: The right of citizens of the United States to vote shall not be denied or abridged by the United States or by any state on account of sex.

10. Knowledge Societies are identified as societies based on the creation, dissemination and utilization of information and knowledge. It is a society with an economy in which knowledge is acquired, created, disseminated and applied to enhance economic and social development.
    http://www.gesci.org/assets/files/2.%20Knowledge%20Society%20Oc tober%202_012.pdf

11. Scientists at Newcastle University in the UK have discovered that girls tend to optimize brain connections earlier than boys. The researchers conclude that this may explain why females generally mature faster in certain cognitive and emotional areas than males during childhood and adolescence. The new study(link is external) was published December 19, 2013 in *Cerebral Cortex.*
    www.psychologytoday.com/blog/the-athletes-way/201312/scientists-identify-why-girls-often-mature-faster-than-boys

12. Francis Fukuyama is Olivier Nomellini Senior Fellow at the Freeman Spogli Institute for International Studies (FSI), and the Director of FSI's Center on Democracy, Development, and the Rule of Law. His book, *The End of History and the Last Man,* was published by Free Press in 1992 and has appeared in over twenty foreign editions. His

172

most recent book, *Political Order and Political Decay: From the Industrial Revolution to the Globalization of Democracy,* was published in September 2014.

13. Four Freedoms Speech: *01/06/1941:* "In the future days, which we seek to make secure, we look for-ward to a world founded upon four essential human freedoms. The first is freedom of speech and expression—everywhere in the world. The second is freedom of every person to worship God in his own way—everywhere in the world. The third is freedom from want—which, translated into world terms, means economic under-standings which will secure to every nation a healthy peacetime life for its inhabitants everywhere in the world. The fourth is free-dom from fear—which, translated into world terms, means a world-wide reduction of armaments to such a point and in such a thorough fashion that no nation will be in a position to commit an act of physical aggression against any neighbor—anywhere in the world." *http://www.fdrlibrary.marist.edu/pdfs/fftext.pdf*

14. Politically active nonprofits – principally those under 501(c)(4) and 501(c)(6) have become a major force in federal elections over the last three cycles. The term "dark money" is often applied to this category of political spender because these groups do not have to disclose the sources of their funding – though a minority do disclose some or all of their donors, by choice or in response to specific circumstances. https://www.opensecrets.org/outsidespending/nonprof_summ.php

15. http://www.nytimes.com/2015/08/06/opinion/america-deserves-a-servant-leader.html?_r=0

16. http://www.forbes.com/sites/realspin/2013/11/24/why-the-u-s-remains-the-worlds-unchallenged-superpower/

17. "The United States is the world leader and likely to remain there for decades. It has the greatest soft power in the world by far. The United States still receives far more immigrants each year (one million) than any other country in the world. The United States leads the world in high technology (Silicon Valley), finance and business (Wall Street), the movies (Hollywood) and higher education (17 of the top 20 universities in the world in Shanghai's Jaotong University survey). The United States has a First World trade profile (massive exports of consumer and technology goods and imports of natural resources)."

18. The Committee on the Present Danger (CPD) is a neoconservative pressure group that aims "to stiffen American resolve to confront the challenge presented by terrorism and the ideologies that drive it." Re-launched in 2004 to focus on the "war on terror," the CPD was initially created during the Cold War by foreign policy hawks who promoted confrontational ant-Soviet policies. Although many ofits 100-plus members continue to publish and organize, particularly around the issue of Iran and its nuclear program, the group has been largely dormant for many years. - See more at: http://www.rightweb.irc-online.org/profile/Committee_on_the_Present_Danger#sthash.fDejTGQt.dpuf

19. http://www.un.org/en/documents/udhr/AMERICA'S MISSION

IX. AMERICA'S PURPOSE

1. Preamble, *Op. cit.*

2. http://rinkworks.com/said/yogiberra.shtml

3. After attending Saint Mary's University of Minnesota for three years, Jack Hennessy enrolled in the United States Military Academy and graduated in 1944, receiving his commission in the infantry. He deployed to the European Theater, serving as a platoon leader and company commander. After an extensive military career, serving in a variety of theaters and moving up the ranks, he received his fourth star and assumed command of the United States Readiness Command at MacDill Air Force Base in December 1974. He retired in 1979 at the end of that tour. After retiring from the Army, Hennessey served on the Board of Trustees of the University of Tampa and was executive director of the Tampa Bay Area Research and Development Authority under the University of South Florida https://en.wikipedia.org/wiki/John_J._Hennessey. A force multiplier refers to a factor that dramatically increases (hence "multiplies") the effectiveness of an item or group. in military usage, it refers to an attribute or a combination of attributes which make a given force more effective than that same force would be without it. The expected size increase required to have the same effectiveness without that advantage is the multiplication factor. For example, if a certain technology like GPS enables a force to accomplish the same results of a force five times as large but without GPS, then the multiplier is five. Such estimates are used to justify an investment cost for force

174

multipliers Some common force multipliers are: Morale; Technology; Geographical features; Weather; Recruitment through diplomacy; Training and experience; Fearsome reputation; Deception; Military strategy, such as the Fabian strategy; Military tactics, such as force concentration. https://en.wikipedia.org/wiki/Force_multiplication

4. www.legacy.com/obituaries/unionleader/obituary.aspx?pid=172260109

5. Wood. *Op cit.*

6. http://www.abrahamlincolnonline.org/lincoln/speeches/congress.htm

7. Dr. Mangosuthu Gatsha Buthelezi (born 1928), played a leading role in South Africa's political history. Founder of the Inkatha Freedom Party (IFP) and heir to the Chieftainship of the Buthelezi tribe, Buthelezi was elected Chief Executive Officer of the KwaZulu Territory in 1970, Chief Executive Councillor of the KwaZulu Legistative Assembly in 1972, and Chief Minister of KwaZulu in 1976. He is also Chancellor of the University of Zululand and was appointed Minister of Home Affairs (1994) in Nelson Mandela's coalition government.
Read more at http://biography.yourdictionary.com/mangosuthu-gatsha-buthelezi#YLesRlgF8I4b1GwY.99

X. HISTORIC DAY

1. Role of President in Constitutional government: "The delegates to the Constitutional Convention of 1787 gave surprisingly little attention to the executive branch of government. In contrast to the protracted debates over the powers of Congress, the powers of the president were defined fairly quickly and without much discussion. This might in part be due to the reluctance of delegates to offend George Washington, the presiding officer of the Convention, and the man all delegates assumed would be the nation's first president."
http://law2.umkc.edu/faculty/projects/ftrials/conlaw/prespowers.html

2. *As You Like It*, Act II, Scene VII [All the world's a stage]

3. T.S. Eliot's "Chorus from the Rock" http://www.tech-samaritan.org/blog/2010/06/16/choruses-from- the-rock-t-s-eliot/

4. www.nytimes.com/learning/general/onthisday/990908onthisdaybig.html

5. This article focuses on the incredible determination of former FBI Special Agent Michael Finnegan, who spent five-plus years of his life studying the activities of Palestinian terrorist Khalid Al-Jawary, tracking him down from country to country through Europe and the Middle East and finally arresting him in Italy, transporting him to the U.S. for trial, and then providing evidence and testimony in court that assured his conviction."
http://gsnmagazine.com/article/42480/fbispecialagentmikefinnegan%E2%80%99srelentlesspursuit

6. Teller, Edward. (1981) *The Pursuit of Simplicity.* Pepperdine University Press, Malibu, CA

7. Actor/director Sam Wanamaker was one of those whose career was nearly derailed by the machinations of Senator McCarthy. He made his feature film debut in My Girl Tisa (1948). The following year, Wanamaker, whose leftist political views were no secret in Hollywood, went to England to appear in blacklisted director Edward Dymtryk's Give Us This Day (1949). After making another film in Britain, Wanamaker learned that he too was about to be investigated and had been blacklisted. Wanamaker elected to remain in England. Over the next ten years, he worked on-stage as a director, producer, and actor. In the 1960s, Wanamaker resumed his acting career in internationally produced films such as The Concrete Jungle (1962) and The Spy Who Came in From the Cold (1965). When not busy acting or directing, Wanamaker had been an active supporter of the plan to restore Shakespeare's Globe Theatre. Unfortunately, Wanamaker died of cancer just before the project was completed.
http://www.fandango.com/samwanamaker/biography/P115914

8. https://www.whitehouse.gov/1600/presidents/Ronaldreagan

9. www.preteristarchive.com/BibleStudies/BibleNT/Luke/luke23-34.html

10. http://avalon.law.yale.edu/19thcentury/lincoln2.asp

11. http://library.timelesstruths.org/music/Amazing_Grace/

XI. TOP TEN

1. Federalist Papers No. 81:
http://www.constitution.org/fed/federa81.htm

2. *How the Supreme Court Responds to Public Opinion* By Erik Voeten "Why would the Court respond to public opinion? Judges are not

elected by the public. Isn't the purpose of a counter-majoritarian institution precisely that it does not follow swings in public mood? Still, political scientists have amassed an impressive array of evidence in favor of the hypothesis that the Court follows changes in public opinion. But why? There are at least three plausible mechanisms. The first, and most obvious, is that public opinion may influence which judges are nominated and confirmed. Second, justices may care about public opinion for a host of reasons that can conveniently be labelled under the rubric "institutional legitimacy." I find a third mechanism more intriguing in terms of interpreting this week's decisions; namely the social-psychological theory that people with more moderate ideological views are more likely to change their views in response to information about what others think. William Mishler and Reginal Sheehan found that: the impact of public opinion is greatest among moderate justices who are likely to hold critical swing positions on the Court." http://www.washingtonmonthly.com/ten-miles-square/2013/06/howthesupremecourtresponds045541.php

3. Preamble, *Op. cit.*

4. http://www.goodreads.com/quotes/68003-to-accept-your-country-without-betraying-it-you-must-love

5. Stephen Colbert quote: http://www.dailykos.com/story/2012/04/28/1087135/-PRICELESS-Colbert-Rips-David-Koch-to-His-Face-at-TIME-Magazine-Gala

6. http://www.telegraph.co.uk/finance/newsbysector/banksandfinancnksandfinance/9561349/Gentle-giant-Paul-Volcker-has-too-little-time-left-to-fix-the-world.html

7. Volker. *Op. cit.*

8. John Jay Federalist Paper No. 2: http://www.constitution.org/fed/federa02.htm

9. https://en.wikipedia.org/wiki/William_P._Rogers

10. http://www.washingtonpost.com/wp-srv/politics/special/watergate/baker.html

11. http://www.investopedia.com/articles/07/new-century.asp

12. W. Sterling Cole: http://www.nytimes.com/1987/03/17/obituaries/w-sterling-cole-82-dies-of-cancer.html

13. Karen Elliott House: Ms. House is former senior vice president of Dow Jones & Company and publisher of the *Wall Street Journal*. Most of

her 32-year career at the *Journal* as a reporter, editor and executive focused on international affairs. She served as diplomatic correspondent, foreign editor and President of Dow Jones' international operations prior to becoming publisher in July 2002. Following joining the *Journal* in 1974, she won numerous awards, including the Pulitzer Prize in international reporting (1984) http://www.cfr.org/staff/b261

14. https://books.google.com/books?id=NxXGFwDhLicC&pg=PA160 &lpg=PA160&dq=John+Gardner+%22Anti-leadership+Vaccine%22&source=bl&ots=TARtVn-FpF&sig=zYFUvdwu82WWZbHL5Z8TzxQxaUE&hl=en&sa=X&ved =0CDoQ6AEwB2oVChMI2vz_4M3-yAIVhlg-Ch3oDgPz#v=onepage&q=John%20Gardner%20%22Anti-Leadership%20Vaccine%22&f=false

15. For a variety of quotes by Thomas Jefferson on education see: http://tjrs.monticello.org/archive/search/quotes?keys=&field_tjrs_cate gorization_tid%5b%5d=2174

16. Allen Carter: http://www.nyu.edu/library/bobst/collections/exhibits/arch/Whoswho/ Frames.html

17. Clark Kerr (1911-2003) was President of the UC system where he spearheaded the negotiation of California's Master Plan for Higher Education, a 1960 document that endures to this day and is considered a model plan by many states and other nations. He went on to lead the influential Carnegie Commission on Higher Education from 1967-1973, and then its successor the Carnegie Council on Policy Issues in Higher Education until 1979. http://www.cshe.berkeley.edu/events/about-clark-kerr

18. *Shabbir Mansuri*: http://www.discoverthenetworks.org/printgroupProfile.asp?grpid=761 7

19. Dr. Catherine Tinker: is the chair of the European Affairs Committee of the New York City Bar Association (2013-2016). She has been a consultant on various projects involving the United Nations and international law, contributing archival research and writing for several publications on the United Nations, including A World in Need of Leadership: Tomorrow's UN, published by the Ford Foundation and the Dag Hammarskjold Foundation; and Crossing the Divide:

Dialogue among Civilizations, by Seton Hall University, http://clecenter.com/Program/ProgramDescription.aspx?pgmid=3906

20. "Ordain" history:"- to appoint or admit to the ministry of the Church," fro stem of stem of Old French ordener "place in order, arrange, prepare; consecrate, designate. Online Etymology Dictionary, © 2010

21. Sam Melville Gibbons was born on Jan. 20, 1920, in Tampa. He practiced law and in 1953 was elected to the Florida House of Representatives, where he served three two-year terms. He then served four years in the State Senate. While in the State Legislature, he helped create the University of South Florida. He managed Senator John F. Kennedy's presidential campaign in Florida. In 1964, when most Florida politicians refused to campaign for President Johnson, he toured the state, making dozens of speeches for the President. Mr. Gibbons retired from Congress in 1996 without ever having lost an election. He was not chairman of Ways and Means long enough for the experience to swell his head. When asked how it felt to be in the chair at one of the most important tables in American politics, he said: "It's like all the other chairs in there. It's kind of hard." http://www.nytimes.com/2012/10/11/us/politics/sam-m-gibbons-florida-congressman-dies-at-92.html?_r=0

22. https://www.goodreads.com/author/quotes/18495.TomBrokaw

23. José Ferrer was born on January 8, 1912 in Santurce, Puerto Rico as José Vicente Ferrer de Otero y Cintrón. He was an actor, known for Lawrence of Arabia (1962), Dune(1984) and The Caine Mutiny (1954). He was married to Stella Daphne Magee,Rosemary Clooney, Phyllis Hill and Uta Hagen. He died on January 26, 1992 in Coral Gables, Florida, USA. His most famous performance was as "Cyrano de Bergerac". He played the role on the stage in 1946 and 1953, on film in 1950 (Cyrano de Bergerac (1950), winning the Oscar for that performance, and on live television in 1949 and 1955. He played Cyrano again in the French film Cyrano et d'Artagnan (1964). He won the Tony for his stage portrayal of the role in 1947, and is one of only nine actors to win the Tony and the Oscar for their performance the same role on Broadway and on film. http://www.imdb.com/name/nm0001207/bio

24. Anne Armstrong was a strong-willed Texas Republican who helped run a working cattle ranch, championed women's rights and served as the United States' first female ambassador to Britain. During the 1970s, Mrs. Armstrong was one of the most prominent women in the Republican Party, became the first woman to address the Republican

National Convention as a keynote speaker and was mentioned as a vice presidential prospect. She was an influential adviser to Presidents Richard M. Nixon, Ronald Reagan and George H.W. Bush, and in 1987 received the Presidential Medal of Freedom, the country's highest civilian award. http://www.washingtonpost.com/wp-dyn/content/article/2008/07/30/AR2008073002605.html

XII. LEARNING NATION

1. http://www.fastcompany.com/36819/learning-change

2. http://www.technologyessays.com/essays/bellspostindustrialsociety essay.htm

3. Mihajlo Mesarovic and Eduard Postel authors http://www.informationclearinghouse.info/article19557.htm

4. Zhao, Yong. (2012) *World Class Learner: Educating Creative & Entrepreneurial Students.* Corwin, Thousand Oaks, CA.

5. Diane Ravitch is Research Professor of Education at New York University and a historian of education. From 1991 to 1993, she was Assistant Secretary of Education and Counselor to Secretary of Education Lamar Alexander in the administration of President George H.W. Bush. She was responsible for the Office of Educational Research and Improvement in the U.S. Department of Education

6. Robert Bannister: http://www.swarthmore.edu/SocSci/rbannis1/vita.html

7. President Obama was elected by large pluralities of minorities.

8. Briane Dumaine, of Fortune magazine wrote: "A group of nearly 400 who gathered last June for a management conference at Bretton Woods, New Hampshire, hail from some of America's largest corporations and most influential consulting firms. What they're celebrating is the learning organization and its intellectual and spiritual champion, Peter Senge. This unassuming, soft-spoken MIT senior lecturer and consultant is the corporate equivalent of a medieval crusader -- a man who, despite heavy odds against his cause, is obsessed with changing not only corporate America but also the world. Senge, who describes himself as an "idealistic

pragmatist," is hard at work building learning organizations. But what exactly is this amorphous creature? The idea, which has been around for years as an academic theory, gained broad currency when Senge published his best-selling The Fifth Discipline in 1990. In it he writes that a learning organization values - and thinks competitive advantage derives from - continuing learning, both individual and collective.
http://archive.fortune.com/magazines/fortune/fortune_archive/1994/10/17/79843/index.htm

9. Jervis never used the term but his meaning embraced it

10. http://www.commongood.org/pages/philip-k.-howard

11. Howard, Phillip K. (2014). *The Rule of Nobody: Saving America from Dead Laws and Broken Government.* W.W. Norton, NY.

12. http://www.washingtonpost.com/wp-dyn/content/article/2009/12/07/AR2009120702241.htm

13. W. Edwards Deming was an adviser, consultant, author, and teacher to some of the most influential businessmen, corporations and scientific pioneers of business process reengineering. He has been described as a national folk hero in Japan, where he was directly responsible for inspiring and guiding the spectacular rise of Japanese industry after World War II, as well as the original management science guru, and founder of the third wave of the Industrial Revolution. His extensive list of published works includes nearly 200 papers, articles, and books.

14. Norman Ornstein and Thomas Mann Explain Why Congress is Failing Us http://billmoyers.com/segment/norman-ornstein-and-thomas-mann-explain-why-congress-is-failing-us/ April 26, 2013. "Political scholars Norman Ornstein and Thomas Mann tell Bill that Congress' failure to make progress on gun control last week — despite support for background checks from 90 percent of the American public — is symptomatic of a legislative branch reduced to dysfunction, partisan ravings and obstruction. Ornstein and Mann say the mainstream media and media fact-checkers add to the problem by indulging in 'false equivalency' — pretending both parties are equally to blame. "Sadly, divided party government . . . is a formula for inaction and absolutist opposition politics, not for problem solving .Some of this is coming from the kinds of people who we're electing to office, through a nominating process that has

gotten so skewed to the radical right. But some of it is an electoral magnet that pulls them away from voting for anything that might have a patina of bipartisan support because they'll face extinction."

XIII. AMERICAN PRAGMATISM

1.   http://engagingpeace.com/?p=6365

2.   The Pope's address to Congress, *Op. cit.*

3.   Noam Chomsky:
      https://raashun.wordpress.com/2013/10/28/terrorism-and-justice-some-useful-truisms-by-noam-chomsky/

4.   http://www.dissidentvoice.org/Articles/Chomsky_TerrorandJusticeResponse.htm

5.   William James was a great thought leader: William James. (1907). *Pragmatism: A New Name for Some Old Ways of Thinking.* Longman Green and Co. New York. In his Pragmatism, William James characterizes truth in terms of usefulness and acceptance. In general, on his view, truth is found by attending to the practical consequences of ideas. To say that truth is mere agreement of ideas with matters of fact, according to James, is incomplete, and to say that truth is captured by coherence is not to distinguish it from a consistent falsity. In a genuine sense, James believes we construct truth in the process of successful living in the world: truth is no sense absolute. Beliefs are considered to be true if and only if they are useful and can be practically applied. At one point in his works, James states, ". . . the ultimate test for us of what a truth means is the conduct it dictates or inspires." Certainly, one difficulty in understanding James lies in the interpretation of his rhetorical flourishes.

6.   http://ecotopia.org/a-moral-equivalent-of-war/ lawof reciprocityexplained

7.   http://www.briantracy.com/blog/sales-success/using-the-law-of-reciprocity-and-other-persuasion-techniques-correctly/

8.   Dodson, Dan W. (1965). *Crisis in the public schools: racial segregation Northern style.* Council for American Unity, New York.

9. http://finance.yahoo.com/news/money-101--q-a- with-warren-buffett-140409456.html

10. "Innovation and Entrepreneurship in a Global Economy." When Peter Drucker wrote about innovation and entrepreneurship in the mid 1980s (*Innovation and Entrepreneurship Principles and Practices*, 1985), America employed 10 million more people than had been predicted, and its dynamic economy was headed toward a primarily entrepreneurially inspired, innovative business culture. . . . Incorporating innovative ideas in business quickly became a highly esteemed management goal worthy of great effort. Corporate executives required their people to learn the disciplines of innovation and entrepreneurship, and Peter Drucker became their teacher. Twenty-five years and one computer revolution later, where do these concepts stand? American business has undergone more extreme changes in every aspect in every industry than could have ever been predicted. Many center on technology, information and productivity, which Drucker steadfastly argued were less important than management.
    http://druckersociety.at/repository/scientific/Pearl.pdfustainable

11. From a NY Times book review: " Zakaria proceeds more subtly than the run-of-the-mill declinist by stressing American advantages not captured by growth rates and export surpluses. He rightly takes on the old saw to the effect that China produces 600,000 engineers a year, India 350,000 and the United States only 70,000. This is true if you include auto mechanics and industrial repairmen in the Asian totals. Subtract them, and America actually trains more engineers per capita than either India or China does."

12. http://www.dce.harvard.edu/professional/blog/paradox-leadership Michael Shinagel, former dean of continuing education and University extension, senior lecturer on English at Harvard University, and instructor of Leadership and Decision Making writes: "Despite the popularity of the topic, leadership remains a paradox. People who seek to understand it by reading a primer on the topic will I inevitably be frustrated and disappointed. Leadership, after all, is an art, not a science. And leadership is not limited to a professional field or industry. Leaders transcend the confines of a defining box. First of all, leaders are not born but evolve into that role. The magic of leadership was best captured by Lao Tzu: *"A leader is best when people barely know he exists, when his work is done, his aim*

fulfilled, they will say: we did it ourselves." This is the art of leadership at its best: the art that conceals art.

13. http://thephilosophersmail.com/perspective/the-great-eastern-philosophers-lao-

14. Edward Luttwak is a CSIS senior associate and has served as a consultant to the Office of the Secretary of Defense, the National Security Council, the U.S. Department of State, the U.S. Army, Navy, and Air Force, and a number of allied governments as well as international corporations and financial institutions. He is a frequent lecturer at universities and military colleges in the United States and abroad and has testified before several congressional committees and presidential commissions. http://csis.org/expert/edward-n-luttwak

15. William James. *Op. cit.*

16. http://wallstreetwindow.com/iron-triangle; "Iron Triangles originated as a means of lobbyists trying to get their point of views conveyed to the government. . . . The concept of an iron triangle derives from sociologist C. Wright Mills's power elite theory. How Does An Iron Triangle Work? It starts with close relationships forming between the government (Federal Congress in case of the U.S.), Federal bureaucratic agencies and interest groups and lobbyists. The interest groups aid the government with useful statistics, information, political support and funding. The agencies gain favorable remarks and testimonials in regards to their services. The government returns the favor by passing laws and policies beneficial to these groups. The agencies help the government in passing these laws easily. Thus, all elements of the triangle keep the others happy and create a mutually sustainable relationship."

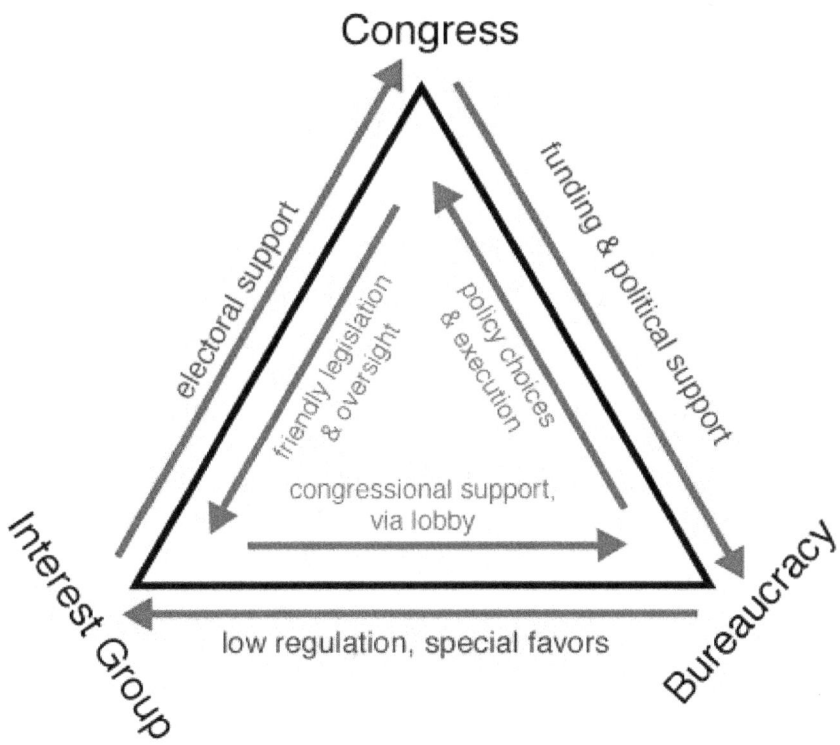

17. For an extensive discussion see:
    http://plato.stanford.edu/entries/smith-moral-political/

18. Pope Francis's address to Congress, *Op. cit.* also:
    https://www.washingtonpost.com/blogs/post-
    partisan/wp/2013/11/26/pope-francis-stinging-critique-of-
    capitalism. "Since Cardinal Jorge Bergoglio became Pope
    Francis in March, the new pontiff has made headlines around
    the world for his emphasis on social and economic equality.
    The first major document of his papacy . . ., is no different.
    Though framed as a call for Catholics to embrace a new
    evangelization, much of "Evangelii Gaudium" is relevant to
    both Catholics and non-Catholics — especially the pope's
    stinging critique of the unequal economy that we live in. He
    writes: 'Just as the commandment "Thou shalt not kill" sets a
    clear limit in order to safeguard the value of human life, today
    we also have to say "thou shalt not" to an economy of exclusion
    and inequality. Such an economy kills. Today everything comes

under the laws of competition and the survival of the fittest, where the powerful feed upon the powerless. As a consequence, masses of people find themselves excluded and marginalized: without work, without possibilities, without any means of escape.'

19. R-E-S-P-E-C-T
    Read more: Aretha Franklin - Respect Lyrics MetroLyrics

20. https://www.biblegateway.com/verse/en/Micah%206%3A8

21. Sari Nusseibeh is Professor of Islamic and Political Philosophy and President of al-Quds University, East Jerusalem (1995-present). He taught at Birzeit University in the West Bank from 1978 until 1991, when he was placed under administrative detention in an Israeli jail for three months. Following his release, he joined his colleagues in the Palestinian negotiating team with Israel, heading the Technical and Advisory committees. At the same time, he co-founded the Fatah Higher Committee in the Occupied Territories, serving as it Deputy Chairman. In 2003, Sari Nusseibeh co-founded IPSO (the Israel/Palestine Scientific Organization), and continues to serve at its co-chairman to this day. http://humctr.jhu.edu/bios/Sari-Nusseibeh/

22. See, for instance: http://www.wrmea.org/2005-april/southern-california-chronicle.html "Under the name American Friends of al-Quds University, a group of concerned Southern Californians agreed to stage fund-raising projects for the only institution of higher learning for Palestinians in Jerusalem. According to Rabia Hussaini, whose husband, Dr. Hatem Hussaini, was the first President of the University, founded in 1994, the institution has a $12 million budget, 70 percent of which depends on tuition. Since more than half of its 8,000 students are unable to cover tuition, it is hoped sources such as AFQU will be able to make up the difference."

.

XIV. MENTAL MAPS

1. Sacks, Oliver. (1985) *The Man Who Mistook his Wife for a Hat.* Touchstone, New York.. Dr. Sacks recounts the case histories of patients lost in the bizarre, apparently inescapable world of neurological disorders: people afflicted with fantastic perceptual and

intellectual aberrations; patients who have lost their memories and with them the greater part of their pasts; who are no longer able to recognize people and common objects; who are stricken with violent tics and grimaces or who shout involuntary obscenities; whose limbs have become alien; who have been dismissed as retarded yet are gifted with uncanny artistic or mathematical talents. . . . They are studies of life struggling against incredible adversity, and they enable us to enter the world of the neurologically impaired, to imagine with our hearts what it must be to live and feel as they do.
http://www.oliversacks.com/books-by-oliver-sacks/man-mistook-wife-hat/

2. Jeffrey Lieberman wraparound services, psychotic symptoms (Jeffrey A. Lieberman "How to Halt the Violence" NYT Aug 29, 2015 Chairman of Psychiatry at the Columbia University Medical Center & author of "Shrinks: The Untold Story of Psychiatry") The New York State Office of Mental Health was an early adopter of an innovative program called OnTrackNY. Similar programs are now spreading across the country and being supported by the federal government. This model of mental health care targets adolescents and young adults in the incipient stages of psychotic disorders and establishes specialized clinics that provide "wraparound" services with pharmacological, psychological, educational and social-support treatments to engage patients and promote recovery.

3. The Rev. Barbara Sloop served as an associate pastor at Second Presbyterian Church in Indianapolis, the largest Presbyterian church in Indiana.. Her own sense of vocation came from working with persons suffering from leprosy and then AIDS, alongside Surgeon General C. Everett Koop. "I began to see," she says, "that for some persons, healing could come only through a relationship with God, and a life beyond this one." Sloop is convinced that the expertise and perspective she gained from her medical career has helped her relationship with Second Presbyterian. . . . On the sociopolitical level, she thinks it's important that "women and people of color are making the ministry more representative of the world."
https://www.washingtonpost.com/archive/opinions/1994/05/15/when-the-minister-is-a-mom/ea5127f9-af3d-45c7-9ad2-bc794e500cf9/

4. http://www.surgeongeneral.gov/about/previous/biokoop.html

5. Pope Francis address to Congress, *Op. cit.*

6. http://www.nytimes.com/2015/05/01/business/hank-greenberg-still-in-the-ring-battling-aig-charges.html?_r=0 "Nothing is more important

than Hank's place in history. Much of that history is on display in Mr. Greenberg's spacious corner office, which is lined with photographs of him with American presidents, cabinet officers and foreign leaders, many of whom Mr. Greenberg has outlived. Mr. Greenberg succeeded Mr. Starr as chief executive in 1967 and took the company public. Before the financial crisis, A.I.G. was the largest insurance company in the world and reached a market capitalization of $242 billion in 2000."

7. As stated in the Chamber's bio: "Thomas J. Donohue is president and CEO of the U.S. Chamber of Commerce. Since assuming this position in 1997, Donohue has built the Chamber into a lobbying and political powerhouse with expanded influence across the globe. Under Donohue's leadership, the Chamber has emerged as a major political force in races for the Senate and the House of Representatives. As part of this bipartisan effort, millions of grassroots business advocates, as well as the Chamber's federation of state and local chambers and industry associations, mobilize in support of pro-business candidates." https://www.uschamber.com/thomas-j-donohue

8. A commentary on Megatrends importance at the time can be found at: http://www.buffalonews.com/did_megatrends_pan_out_a_look_back_ at_societal_predictions_30_years_later.html As we move from an industrial to an information society, we will use our brainpower to create instead of our physical power … it is a great and yeasty time, filled with opportunity … My God, what a fantastic time to be alive!" John Naisbitt, in his conclusion of "Megatrends."

9. Robert "Bob" Martinez (born December 25, 1934) was the 40th Governor of Florida from 1987 to 1991; he was the first person of Spanish ancestry to be elected to the state's top office. Prior to that, he was the mayor of Tampa from 1979 to 1986. After leaving the governor's office on January 8, 1991, Martinez was appointed by President George H. W. Bush to the cabinet rank position of Director of the Office of National Drug Control Policy (or "Drug Czar") where he served until January 20, 1993.Since then, Martinez has served as a consultant to Florida-based businesses and law firms and is a political analyst for Bay News 9 television. He is a trustee of the University of Tampa, and a director of the Hillsborough Education Foundation, Tampa's Lowry Park Zoo and the Tampa Bay History Center, all local nonprofit groups involved in some way with education. https://en.wikipedia.org/wiki/Bob_Martinez

10. Pope Francis address to Congress. *Op. cit.*

XV. ACCOUNTABLE NOW

1. Einstein's equation $E=mc^2$ pops up on everything from <u>baseball</u> caps to bumper stickers. It's even the title of a 2008 Mariah Carey album. But what does Albert Einstein's famous equation really mean? For starters, the **E** stands for **energy** and the **m** stands for **mass**, a measurement of the quantity of matter. Energy and matter are interchangeable. Furthermore, it's essential to remember that there's a set amount of energy/matter in the universe. . . . . The grand total remains constant, but energy regularly changes form into matter and matter into energy. Now we're getting to the c^2 part of the equation. The **c** stands for the **speed of light**, a universal constant, so the whole equation breaks down to this: Energy is equal to matter multiplied by the speed of light squared. The speed of light squared is a colossal number, illustrating just how much energy there is in even tiny amounts of matter. A common example of this is that 1 gram of water -- if its whole mass were converted into pure energy via $E=mc^2$ — contains as much energy as 20,000 tons (18,143 metric tons) of TNT exploding. That's why such a small amount of uranium or plutonium can produce such a massive atomic explosion. Einstein's equation opened the door for numerous technological advances, from nuclear power and nuclear medicine to the inner workings of the sun. It shows us that matter and energy are one. http://science.howstuffworks.com/science-vs-myth/everyday-myths/einstein-formula.htm

2. **1609** - Johannes Kepler uses the dark night sky to argue for a finite universe. Kepler discovered the key to building a heliocentric model. The planets moved in ellipses, not perfect circles, about the Sun - known as the Laws of planetary motion. Newton later showed that elliptical motion could be explained by his inverse-square law for the gravitational force. **1609** - Galileo Galilei observes moons of Jupiter in support of the heliocentric model. (Heliocentrism is the theory that the Sun is at the center of the Universe and/or the Solar System. The word is derived from the Greek (Helios = "Sun" and kentron = "Center")). **1687** - Newton: Laws of motion, law of universal gravitation, basis for classical physics. http://www.spaceandmotion.com/cosmology-history-astronomy-universe-space.htm

3. Brian Greene stressed this in his 100th anniversary article: http://www.worldsciencefestival.com/participants/briangreene/

4. Sir James Jeans "God is a mathematician."
   https://books.google.com/books?id=RNwnUL33epsC&pg=PA58&lpg
   =PA58&dq=ir+James+Jeans+%E2%80%9CGod+is+a+mathematician
   +%E2%80%94The+Mysterious+Universe,+1930&source=bl&ots=P94
   rW_53Ob&sig=FRMLLPa8hW_DQi0NeaawoWv1Ppc&hl=en&sa=X
   &ved=0CEsQ6AEwCGoVChMI4rPWh5iCyQIVyuwmCh3F0wUk#v=
   onepage&q=Sir%20James%20Jeans%20%E2%80%9CGod%20is%20
   a%20mathematician%20%E2%80%94The%20Mysterious%20Univers
   e%2C%201930&f=false

5. "The Rock" by T.S. Eliot
   http://www.rjgeib.com/thoughts/information/information.html

6. Hamilton. Federalist Papers
   http://avalon.law.yale.edu/18th_century/fed70.asp

7. Hamilton. #70 *Op.cit.*

8. On June 16, 185. Lincoln delivered this address to his Republican colleagues in the Hall of Representatives. The title reflects part of the
   speech's introduction, "A house divided against itself cannot stand," a
   concept familiar to Lincoln's audience is that statement by Jesus
   recorded in all three synoptic gospels (Matthew, Mark, Luke).8. Mark
   3:25 New Testament.
   http://www.abrahamlincolnonline.org/lincoln/speeches/house.htm

9. http://biblehub.com/luke/11-17.htm

10. David M. Abshire cofounded CSIS in 1962, serving as its chief
    executive for many years, and is currently vice chairman of the board.
    He cofounded the CSIS Abshire-Inamori Leadership Academy in 2002
    with Kazuo Inamori. Dr. Abshire received a Ph.D. in history from
    Georgetown University, where he also served as an adjunct professor
    at its School of Foreign Service. His government service includes
    assistant secretary of state for congressional relations (1970–1973),
    head of the National Security Group under President Ronald Reagan
    (1980), U.S. ambassador to NATO (1983–1987), and special counselor
    to President Reagan (1987). Dr. Abshire also served as a member of
    the Murphy Commission on the Organization of the Government, the
    President's Foreign Intelligence Advisory Board, the President's Task
    Force on U.S. Governmental International Broadcasting. He has been
    decorated by seven heads of government and is the author of seven
    books. http://csis.org/expert/history-david-m-abshire

11. Dwight Eisenhower's observation was prescient.
    http://www.occupyepa.com/occupy-dod-and-military-industrial-complex.html

12. Howard, Phillip. (2011). *The Death of Common Sense: How Law Is Suffocating America.* Random House, New York.

13. Dr. Sally Ride studied at Stanford University before beating out 1,000 other applicants for a spot in NASA's astronaut program. After rigorous training, Ride joined the Challenger shuttle mission on June 18, 1983, and became the first American woman in space. Ride beat out 1,000 other applicants for a spot in the National Aeronautics and Space Administration's (NASA) astronaut program. She got her chance to go into space and the record books in 1983. After NASA, Ride became the director of the California Space Institute at the University of California, San Diego, as well as a professor of physics at the school in 1989. In 2001, she started her own company to create educational programs and products known as Sally Ride Science to help inspire girls and young women to pursue their interests in science and math. Ride served as president and CEO.

14. Latin teachers at Hempstead H.S. (N.Y.)

15. Drucker, Peter. Post Capitalist Society. p. 83.

16. Dr. Dan W. Dodson, a Texas sharecropper's son who submitted his sun-baked boyhood prejudices to such a searing intellectual analysis that he became one of the nation's leading advocates of racial equality.He was a professor of sociology at New York University. Known as the philosopher of intergroup relations for the torrent of scholarly research papers he produced as director of the N.Y.U. Center for Human Relations Studies, Dr. Dodson did more than provide the theoretical underpinnings for the movement to achieve racial and ethnic harmony. In 1944, he took a leave from the university to serve four years as executive director of the new Mayor's Committee on Unity. Largely because of his work, the committee, which was formed by Mayor Fiorello H. La Guardia to deal with intergroup conflicts, became a model for Federal, state and municipal human rights commissions that proliferated two decades later.
    http://www.nytimes.com/1995/08/19/obituaries/dan-w-dodson-88-foe-and-scholar-of-racism.html

17. For sociological impact, Jack Roosevelt Robinson was perhaps America's most significant athlete. As the first black player in major-league baseball, he was a pioneer. His skill and accomplishments

resulted in the acceptance of blacks in other major sports, notably professional football and professional basketball. He was elected to baseball's Hall of Fame in 1962
http://www.nytimes.com/learning/general/onthisday/bday/0131.html

XVI. AMERICAN SPIRIT

1. https://www.goodreads.com/author/quotes/41343.PaulTillich

2. *Space is not empty. It is full, a plenum as opposed to a vacuum, and is the ground for the existence of everything, including ourselves. The universe is not separate from this cosmic sea of energy."* — David Bohm. David Bohm was one of the most distinguished theoretical physicists of his generation, and a fearless challenger of scientific orthodoxy. His interests and influence extended far beyond physics and embraced biology, psychology, philosophy, religion, art, and the future of society. Underlying his innovative approach to many different issues was the fundamental idea that beyond the visible, tangible world there lies a deeper, implicate order of undivided wholeness. Bohm, an idealist, became involved in politics and he was labeled a communist by the FBI led by J. Edgar Hoover. This prevented him from getting a clearance to work with Oppenheimer on the Manhattan Project at Los Alamos to produce the first atomic bomb during the World War II. However, while working on his doctorate at Berkeley, he discovered "the scattering calculations of collisions of protons and deuterons" which was used by the Manhattan Project team, and was immediately classified.
http://www.scienceandnonduality.com/david-bohm-implicate-order-and-holomovement/
See more at: http://www.scienceandnonduality.com/david-bohm-implicate-order-and-holomovement/#sthash.tud5HmvV.dpuf story

3. pixar.wikia.com/wiki/ToInfinityandBeyond

4. https://www.quora.com/What-did-Einstein-mean-when-he-said-Science-without-religion-is-lame-religion-without-science-is-blind-And-do-you-agree-with-him

5. Robert W. Galvin, took the reins of Motorola from his father and built a family-run business that pioneered Depression-era car radios and wartime walkie-talkies Into a global maker of color television sets, cellphones and other ubiquities of the electronic age. One of America's most visionary entrepreneurs, the keys to success, he often said, were

the foresight to exploit new markets; diversified, high-quality product lines; and progressive management. He practiced them by giving priority to new technologies, moving into Asian and European markets, enforcing quality controls and customer-satisfaction goals, and establishing early profit-sharing plans for employees. In the three decades after Mr. Galvin took control in the late 1950s, annual sales leaped to $10.8 billion from $290 million. http://www.nytimes.com/2011/10/13/technology/robert-w-galvin-who-led-motorola-dies-at-89.html?_r=0

6. Akio Morita, was the co-founder of the Sony Corporation who personified Japan's rise from postwar rubble to industrial riches and became the unofficial ambassador of its business community to the world. http://www.nytimes.com/1999/10/04/business/akio-morita-co-founder-of-sony-and-japanese-business-leader-dies-at-78.html?pagewanted=all

7. http://www.goodreads.com/quotes/24700-the-future-ain-t-what-it-used-to-be

8. Heilbroner, Robert.(1960)*The Future as History*. Harper Collins, New York.

9. http://www.imdb.com/name/nm0000095/bio

10. On a rainy September 13, 1814, British warships sent a downpour of shells and rockets onto Fort McHenry in Baltimore Harbor, relentlessly pounding the American fort for 25 hours. A week earlier, Francis Scott Key, a 35-year-old American lawyer, had boarded the flagship of the British fleet on the Chesapeake Bay in hopes of persuading the British to release a friend who had recently been arrested. Key's tactics were successful, but because he and his companions had gained knowledge of the impending attack on Baltimore, the British did not let them go. Key watched on September 13 as the barrage of Fort McHenry began eight miles away. "It seemed as though mother earth had opened and was vomiting shot and shell in a sheet of fire and brimstone," Key wrote later. But when darkness arrived, Key saw only red erupting in the night sky. Given the scale of the attack, he was certain the British would win. The hours passed slowly, but in the clearing smoke of "the dawn's early light" on September 14, he saw the American flag—not the British Union Jack—flying over the fort, announcing an American victory. Key put his thoughts on paper while still on board the ship, setting his words to the tune of a popular English song. The *Baltimore Patriot* newspaper soon printed it, and within weeks, Key's poem, now called "The Star-Spangled Banner," appeared in print across the

country, immortalizing his words—and forever naming the flag it celebrated
Read more: http://www.smithsonianmag.com/history/the-story-behind-the-star-spangled-banner-149220970/#mWKrcIwMPl4hP5L6.99

11. https://www.archives.gov/education/lessons/day-of-infamy/

12. http://articles.sun-sentinel.com/2001-10-28/entertainment/0110260564_1_pearl-harbor-tora-tora-r

13. http://www.newworldencyclopedia.org/entry/Abrahamic_religions

14. Pope Francis. *Op. cit.*

XVII. CLOSING DEAL

1. http://www.cbsnews.com/news/vladimir-putin-russian-president-60-minutes-charlie-rose/

2. A business metric is a quantifiable measure businesses use to track, monitor and assess the success or failure of various business processes. The main goal of measuring business metrics is to track cost management, but the overall point of employing them is to communicate a company's progression toward certain long- and short-term objectives. This often requires the input of key stakeholders in the business as to which metrics matter to them. Some organizations outline business metrics in mission statements, which require buy-in from all levels of the company, while others simply incorporate them int0 their general workflows.   .
http://searchcrm.techtarget.com/definition/business-metric

3. For example the assessment of quality of life measurements: *AQoL*. See: www.aqol.com.au/

INDEX ~ *The Indomitable Freedom Quest*

Brokaw, Tom, 110
Brooklyn Dodgers, 147
Buffett, Warren, 124
Bush, President George H.W., 137
Butterfly Effect, 56, 57, 149

196

Luttwak, Edward, 126

M
Madison, James, 17, 79
Magna Carta, 29, 78
Mandela. Nelson, 89
Mankind at the Turning Point, (Club of Rome), 74, 114
Mann, Thomas, 119
Mansuri, Shabbir, 108
Mass (m),156
Mass Leadership, 158
Martinez, Bob, 136
McCarthy, Senator Joseph, 148
McCord, Sue, 58
McFadyan-Ketchum, Linda, 9
Mega crisis, 105, 114, 153
Megatrends, (Naisbitt, John), 135
Meta crisis, 153
Meta force, 11, 20, 23, 24, 153
Mental model of the American nation, 57
Moral equivalent of war, 121, 152
Morita, Akio, 150
Morrice, Brad, 103
Morris, Gouverneur, 79
Moses, Jesus, Mohamed, 152
Mutuality, 66

N
Naisbitt, John, 135
National Executive Service Corps, 68
National Institutes of Health, 132
National Purpose,82, 85, 94
Nelson, Suzanne, 58
New Century Financial, 103
New Leadership Ethic, 152
New York University, 107, 123, 147
New York Yankees, 30, 73
Nineteenth Amendment, 80
Nixon, President Richard, 93
Nth commandment, 65, 102, 129, 179
Nucleus, 156
Nusseibeh, Sari, 129

O
Obama, Barack, 18, 22, 116, 128

World War III, 40
Wraparound services, 132

X

Y
Young, Neil, 28

Z
Zakaria, Fareed, 125, 143
Zhao, Yong, (*World Class Learners*), 114

ABOUT THE AUTHOR

Dr. Richard D. Cheshire is a leadership organizer. His career has been about the practice and teaching of transformative leadership, as a college administrator and professor, president of The University of Tampa, author of *Leading by Heart*, vice president for development of the Center for Strategic & International Studies, executive director of the Shakespeare Globe Centre of North America, and a co-founder of the Council for Advancement and Support of Education. He holds that winning hearts and minds works by the same principles in macro-international affairs as in micro-interpersonal relations, and that these principles are universal, the essence of civic virtue among all peoples. His degrees are from Colgate University, the University of New Hampshire, and New York University. He is married, with three children, eight grandchildren, and two great grandchildren.

Vantine Imaging, Hamilton, NY

ACKNOWLEDGMENTS

This book would not have been written without the friendly urging and tireless editing of Arthur Rashap from Charlottesville, Virginia. It would not have taken shape without the straightforward advice and informed experience of Gordon Weil from Harpswell, Maine. The early comments of Andrea Perham from Middlebury, Vermont made a real difference in the way it was conceived. It was composed and compiled with the technical support and instructive expertise of Alamgir Khan now from El Paso, Texas. It was produced with the thoughtful attention and dedicated efforts of Joshua Cheshire from Denver, Colorado. Thank you to them all. Unattributed thoughts and expressions are the full responsibility of the author.

www.ingramcontent.com/pod-product-compliance
Lightning Source LLC
Chambersburg PA
CBHW062146280526
45788CB00001B/325